EMPRESS RISING

EMPRESS RISING

Own Your Energy,
Trust Your Wisdom &
Rewrite the Rules of Aging

ROSE WIPPICH

Published by Spirit Feather Press

The information in this book is for educational and inspirational purposes only and is not intended as medical, psychological, or therapeutic advice. The author is not a licensed healthcare professional. Always consult your physician or qualified healthcare provider before beginning any new wellness practice or if you have medical concerns.

For more information or to request permission, email: rose@rosewippich.com.

Paperback: ISBN 979-8-9997321-0-1
First Paperback Edition August 2025

Book typeset in Astrid, Noto Serif, and Slippery.
Cover & Interior Design by Jane Clark at BrandSwan
Author Photo by Rosalie Marie Photography

The author and publisher disclaim liability for any adverse effects resulting from the use of information in this book. Individual results may vary, and readers assume full responsibility for their health and safety when implementing any practices discussed herein.

This Book is Dedicated

To the women who showed me what it truly means to
embody Empress energy, to other Empresses rising beside me,
and to all the future Empresses we're inspiring along the way.

To my family — I love you.
Thank you for your unwavering support, your belief in me,
and the love that carries me forward.

CONTENTS

Welcome to Your Empress Years

YOUR INVITATION

Something powerful is stirring. Across the world, women in their fifties and beyond are embracing a new narrative about aging. Speaking with more confidence. Shining with inner radiance. Where society once expected them to fade into the background, they are stepping boldly into the spotlight. They are discovering their rightful place not as fading figures, but as vibrant sources of wisdom, power, and purpose — reclaiming the magnificence that was always theirs.

This is the Empress rising — a transformation in how we view, experience, and embody the later chapters of a woman's life.

At sixty-one years young, I found myself reflecting on society's limited vision for women in their wisdom years. The term *crone* kept surfacing in my mind, along with its withered and wrinkled image. Something about this traditional label felt deeply misaligned with the vibrant energy I felt within myself and observed in other women my age. What crystallized in my mind instead was an *Empress* — regal, wise, and radiating power.

This isn't just about replacing a label. It's about a complete re-branding of this phase of *life*. The term *crone* — traditionally referring to a wise elder woman — has become associated with images of a withered, hunched figure. I wanted to honor the wisdom aspect while replacing these outdated visuals with something that reflects what I feel in myself and observe in other Empresses around me. We aren't diminishing with age — we are expanding. We aren't fading — we are in full bloom, or, better yet, still blooming. We are not becoming invisible — we are becoming even more radiant. And it's time we claimed our thrones.

A Collective Awakening

For too long, our culture has offered a limited vision of what aging means for women — suggesting that our most vibrant, impactful, and visible years are behind us. But what if the opposite were true? What if these wisdom years are actually when we come into our fullest power, our deepest wisdom, and our most authentic expression?

Empress Rising is both an invitation and a guidebook for women who sense their growing potential. It's for every woman who has ever walked into a room and felt suddenly overlooked. For every woman who has been passed over, talked over, or expected to step aside. For every woman who intuitively knows that her greatest contributions and most meaningful experiences still lie ahead.

I warmly invite you to join me — and countless other Empresses — on this transformative journey. Together we'll explore how to reclaim our power, trust our intuitive wisdom, and create lives of remarkable purpose in these precious wisdom years. This is a path that we walk together, straightening each other's crowns along the way. As you turn these pages, imagine yourself surrounded by a circle of women who understand, who see you, and who celebrate your rising. The throne that awaits you is part of a greater kingdom we're building together — one where our collective wisdom creates ripples of change far beyond ourselves.

This book is your personal guide to embodying the Empress energy. Each chapter offers both wisdom and practical tools — what I call "Royal Invitations" — exercises, journal prompts, meditations, and rituals that will help you integrate these teachings into your daily life. You might read it cover to cover, or you may open to a page that offers exactly the wisdom you need in that moment. The transformation begins the moment you decide to claim your throne.

Eight Pillars of Empress Energy

As you journey through these pages, you'll explore eight essential themes that form the foundation of the Empress path:

1. **Sovereignty and Personal Power**: Claiming authority over your life, setting boundaries, and recognizing your inherent worth and power.

2. **Transformation and Reinvention**: Embracing opportunities to reinvent yourself, try new things, and transform your approach to life.

3. **Self-Care and Nurturing**: Prioritizing your own well-being after years of caring for others.

4. **Intuitive Wisdom**: Developing and trusting your inner guidance and the deep knowing that comes from life experience.

5. **Energy Management and Protection**: Learning to protect your energy and be selective about where you direct your attention.

6. **Abundance and Gratitude**: Recognizing abundance beyond material wealth and practicing gratitude as a transformative practice.

7. **Forgiveness and Healing**: Exploring how forgiveness becomes a crucial component of freedom and healing in the wisdom years.

8. **Community and Supporting Other Women**: Creating communities that celebrate rather than diminish women's collective wisdom and power.

Empress Rising isn't just a book — it's a movement toward a new understanding of feminine wisdom. It's part of a greater awakening — a collective recognition of divine feminine energy across the world. Women are rediscovering their wisdom, their power, and their essential role as guides and mentors rather than elders who are dismissed.

I've learned that true empowerment comes not from external validation but from inner connection. By writing this book, I've stepped fully into my own energy and sovereignty — trusting my wisdom even when cultural messages suggested I should be stepping back. When we own our energy, we gain the freedom to define this phase of life on our own terms. We can create new, more fulfilling patterns for aging.

As you turn these pages, my deepest wish is that you will feel a power rising within you — gracious, wise, divine, respected, heard, and valued. That you will recognize the jewels in your own crown, accumulated through every triumph and challenge of your life. That you will claim your throne not with arrogance, but with the quiet confidence of a woman who knows her worth.

And if you're already wearing your Empress crown, I hope you'll reach out to others still finding their way. Our individual rising becomes revolutionary when we rise together.

The world needs your wisdom. It needs your voice. It needs your unique gifts that can only come from a life fully lived.

With sovereignty and grace,

Rose

"I always wanted to be a princess. Instead, I've become an Empress."

CHAPTER 1

EMPRESS RISING: FROM CRONE TO CROWN

Traditionally, the crone represents the third aspect of the divine feminine within the Triple Goddess archetype — a woman who has moved beyond her childbearing years and entered the most enlightened stage of her life. Throughout history, she has also been depicted as a teacher, shaman, healer, and wise woman.

The true essence of the crone includes the following:

- Wisdom cultivated through life's rich experiences
- Turning challenges into strength
- Deep connection to intuition and deep spiritual knowledge
- Liberation from society's restraints and expectations
- Guardianship of rituals, traditions, and ancestral knowledge
- Graceful understanding of life's complete cycle

We can still embody these characteristics, but it's time to put an end to the idea of a hunched and withered crone relegated to the shadows of society. It is time because we don't wither and fade when we get to a certain age or when we go through menopause. Instead, we have the energetic sovereignty to rewrite the script of our life. We are not diminishing with age, we are expanding. We are not fading or withering; in fact, we are in full bloom, or better yet, still blooming.

Let us transform the narrative and embrace our rightful title as Empress, the embodiment of the divine feminine in her most powerful manifestation.

The Rise of the Empress

Today, we rise as Empresses — women who have gathered wisdom through our years and wear our experiences with pride. This isn't merely a change of title; it's a reclamation of our power, a revolution in how we see ourselves and how the world perceives us. In essence, we are rebranding ourselves, much like companies do when they want to update a product or change their messaging.

The shift from crone to Empress represents more than just a change in terminology. It's about acknowledging and claiming the full power and potential of women in their mature years. The Empress archetype better captures the combination of wisdom, abundance, power, and active engagement that characterizes women in this phase of their life.

This transformation is gaining momentum worldwide. Across the globe, women in their wisdom years are refusing to accept society's diminished expectations. They're starting businesses, pursuing education, traveling solo, finding love, and discovering passions they never knew existed. These women understand that their accumulated wisdom, emotional intelligence, and freedom from earlier life constraints create the perfect conditions for their most authentic and powerful chapter yet.

I've embraced each transition or phase of my life as an opportunity for growth. I've also met and spoken to many women in their mature years who have been unstoppable on their path to personal power. We can start new careers, lead organizations, mentor others, create positive change, and still enjoy abundance and vitality. It's time to step away from hearing someone else's narrative about what they think we should do and step onto our own throne.

Perhaps you've experienced a moment when you walk into a room and notice younger eyes looking past you and not at you. Does this subtle dismissal make you feel invisible? Or have you found yourself steered toward a conversation revolving around physical ailments and recent medical diagnosis rather than your rich experiences and wisdom? Maybe you've encountered those tired stereotypes: the technology-challenged elder or the woman who sits around and knits all day.

In all honestly, I find these portrayals inadequate and offensive. For one, I am proud of how I navigate technology with confidence and curiosity. I know plenty of people who are much younger and struggle with technology far more than I do. And two, I'm active and energetic with plans to remain so for as long as possible. But there also have been times when I have felt the stigma of aging fall heavily upon me. I notice the passing of my youthful appearance as I look in the mirror and see new wrinkles or the drooping of my eyelids. The experience of "feeling" my age versus "seeing" my age is totally different. When I look out into the world I don't feel my age; I feel youthful, vibrant, sexy, and aligned with my purpose in life. What I feel is a radiance that begins deep within. I nurture this inner flame so it glows brightly enough that others can sense it when they meet me. They perceive beyond my physical appearance, recognizing someone with purpose, dignity, and a fervent desire to live life to the fullest, never blending into the background.

Social media fails to capture the true essence of grace, vitality, and magnificence that comes with this stage of life. I have learned to unlike, scroll past, and ignore how women are being portrayed and, instead, embrace and embody a new way of feeling. We need to embody an energy so authentic and powerful that it transforms every room we enter. Our value isn't found or measured in social media likes or follows. It comes from the experience we've gathered and the strength and resilience we've gained from the challenges that we've faced.

We cannot control how society views aging women or how algorithms favor youth. Society (or should I say influencers and marketing executives) will continue to ignore or push aside older women. It is up to us to ignore what they are doing and become our own influencers. We decide how we want to show up and how we want to be seen. We do this by embodying the Empress energy and leading other women to their thrones. Together, we create community. We create change by rewriting the rules. We have done it before and we will do it again.

Throughout history, women have persistently challenged and dismantled barriers in male-dominated societies. This fight required tremendous courage. Women who simply conformed to societal expectations would never have won basic rights like voting, property ownership, or professional opportunities. The suffragettes, early female scientists and doctors, business pioneers, and countless other women had to face ridicule, discrimination, and often serious personal and professional consequences to create change. While significant progress has been made, many obstacles remain across professional, political, and social spheres.

These women not only broke barriers themselves but often created programs, organizations, or movements to help others follow. Many have used their platforms to advocate for systemic changes beyond their immediate fields, recognizing that progress requires changing both policies and cultural attitudes.

Those of us who have lived through decades of these transformations carry unique wisdom. Women in their mature years have witnessed firsthand how collective action creates change and understand deeply what it means to navigate and challenge patriarchal systems. This lived experience is invaluable. By embracing our earned wisdom and authority — our Empress energy — we can serve as bridges between generations, mentoring younger women while holding space for their fresh perspectives and approaches. Our years of experience allow us to share not just strategies for success but also the emotional resilience and inner strength required for sustained advocacy. We can share our experiences and wisdom, and support one another as women continue to break down barriers and create more opportunities for those who follow. This ongoing work honors both the legacy of those who fought before us and our own power to shape the future. And we can inspire younger women to look forward to their Empress years.

We stand at a magnificent threshold. Behind us lies the maidens we once were, dancing in the spring of youth, and the mothers we became, nurturing life. But now, before us lies a realm of potential. We are entering our sovereignty — our Empress years. The

Empress years are when we can choose to truly and fully express our uniqueness and our gifts. When we no longer feel tethered by society's criticisms or judgments but free of them. We are still youthful in our desire to embrace life to the fullest, but now we appreciate everything much more. We are grateful for the new experiences and for what shaped us. As Empresses, we aren't trying to defy age. We are embodying an energy that is so authentic and powerful that it transforms every room we enter.

The Empress Archetype

I have chosen the Empress archetype because she captures the essence of this magnificent phase in our lives, embodying all that we are becoming. A traditional definition of an Empress is that she is the ruler of an empire or personal kingdom. She is a woman who rules in her own right.

The tarot has dedicated a card to the Empress — an image of a woman sitting on a throne with a harvest of abundance around her. She has lived a full life of riches and experiences, and now she enjoys the fruits of her labor.

She is wise and intuitive, sharing her wisdom with those who ask for it. She is grounded. She is content. She understands that she has an active and important part to play in this world. She knows that her voice and expression is that of experience and wisdom, and she is free to express what she desires. She doesn't force her opinion on others. She inherently knows that she has value.

She is kind and compassionate but also fierce and strong. She has faced many battles with perseverance, strength, and love, and emerged victorious. She has also created many paths or reinvented herself and continues to do so. She understands that her time on this earth is as important as anyone else's — no matter their age. She has arrived at a time in her life when she can sit on her throne, grateful for her abundant life, yet still have several things she wants to conquer. She is an Empress.

An Empress is:

- Regal in her presence. She understands that true power comes from inner confidence rather than external validation. She moves beyond people pleasing and stands in her own power and authenticity. She understands the importance of protecting her own energy.

- Graceful in her power. She understands that true strength lies in knowing when to act and when to observe. She leads by example and inspires others. She embraces change as a pathway to growth and transformation.

- Wise in her decisions. Her choices are informed by years of experience and careful observation. She is discerning and not impulsive. Her wisdom comes from both successes and failures and understanding that both are valuable teachers.

- Nurturing in her strength. She uses her power to uplift others while maintaining healthy boundaries. She knows when to provide support to others and when to let others grow through their own challenges while always being ready to offer a sacred space.

- Sovereign in her domain. Whether her kingdom is a corporation or a cozy home, she presides over it with clear intention and purpose. She creates from a place of possibilities and an abundant and grateful mindset.

This book doesn't explore or imitate historical Empresses or invoke ancient deities. This book is about the Empress that **you** are becoming. The words on these pages are meant to transform how you see yourself and fully embody the Empress that already resides within you.

This archetype speaks to you directly — it doesn't matter what your age is, where you are on this journey, or what others want for you. You deserve to feel amazing and live your best life. You've earned the right to own your power and make choices that align with your divine feminine energy — an energy that may have been put aside or forgotten because of your life's experiences. You are worthy, beautiful, and have so much to offer within your regal, graceful, wise, and strong sovereign self.

Becoming an Empress begins with shifting your perspective and understanding that you are worthy and meant to live an extraordinary life — one in which your desires can become a reality. Don't let limiting beliefs hold you back. Whether you're just beginning this journey or have been walking this path for years, you can reinvent yourself, rewrite your narrative, and step confidently onto the regal red carpet of your amazing journey. It's never too late to:

- Recognize your inherent worth and trust the wisdom that comes with your journey and lived experiences.

- Reinvent yourself. You can start fresh, find a new purpose and blaze new paths.

- Explore new passions or reignite old ones. Get curious and step outside of your comfort zone. Have fun, explore new places, connect with new people, and try new things. Find what lights you up.

- Set empowering boundaries. When you establish personal energetic boundaries, you are making a statement to others and to yourself that you are important.

- Build your circle of support. Surround yourself with people who celebrate your wisdom, honor your boundaries and encourage your growth.

This book is part of a greater awakening — a collective rising of divine feminine energy — that is also deeply personal. You are being asked to claim your seat on the throne of your own kingdom. You carry within you a treasure chest of experiences, wisdom, and gifts that the world desperately needs. Yet before you can share all of this, you must first recognize these gifts within your own sovereignty.

Each chapter offers methods to transform your perspective on aging and embrace and embody a revitalized mindset. This journey isn't merely about reframing your perspective — it's about reclaiming your majesty. As you turn these pages, you'll discover how to transform society's outdated narratives about feminine aging into a celebration of your accumulated power, intuition, and magnificent presence.

The path of the Empress acknowledges that your most influential and radiant years may well be these. When you've gathered the courage to rule your life with authenticity, when your voice carries the weight of lived experience, and when your very presence commands reverence not despite your years, but because of them, then you are indeed an Empress.

My intention for this book is that it serves as a guide, offering you a personalized experience on the journey to discovering what it truly means to embody the Empress energy. My wish is that you will feel a power rising within you — gracious, wise, divine, respected, seen, heard and valued. This transformation happens whether others recognize it or not, because the most powerful validation comes from within.

If you're already wearing an Empress crown, I hope that you'll invite other women into your kingdom and offer them support and guidance. Extend your hand to those who may not yet recognize their royal nature. Share your wisdom through compassionate conversations, thoughtful mentorship, and living as an inspiring example. When you see a sister struggling to reclaim her power, gently remind her of the strength that resides within.

Together, we form a magnificent community of Empresses united in our refusal to fade into invisibility. We become a collective movement of women who are not yet done with living our lives with purpose and meaning, who recognize that our wisdom years may well be our most powerful.

Embodying Empress Energy

An Empress understands that time on this earth is precious and unknown. She doesn't waste it trying to conform to others' expectations or by diminishing her light to make others comfortable. Instead, she does the following:

- Curates her kingdom (life) with discernment, carefully choosing who and what deserves a place in her sacred space. She understands that every yes to something that doesn't align with her values is a no to something that does. Her boundaries are not walls but elegant gates that protect her energy and peace.

- Manifests what serves her highest good by aligning her actions with her deepest truth. She lives her life on purpose. She has learned from her experiences that what she manifests may arrive in unexpected forms that serve her perfectly.

- Nurtures her kingdom (body, mind, and spirit) with royal attention. She recognizes that self-care is essential and not selfish. She knows when to rest and restore her energy. She continues to learn new things and keeps her mind active. And she has a personal spiritual practice that keeps her grounded.

- Inspires other women through her authentic power and understands that how she lives her life can influence and motivate others. Her personal journey serves as a map for others who are ready to navigate transitions, shed outdated beliefs, and embrace a new way of living.

- Carries herself with natural dignity and grace and is true to herself. She laughs often, knowing that laughter is healing. She knows when to remain quiet, understanding that silence has something to say. She is unapologetic in her authenticity and appreciates and honors everything in her life that brought her to the present.

- Embraces her sensuality and doesn't let society dictate how she should feel or how she should express her feminine energy. She understands that she deserves to feel good and explore richer experiences.

- Protects her energy like a precious resource. She knows that not every invitation needs to be accepted. She also knows that she doesn't have to intervene every time a situation or crises arises or offer her opinion when it may not be welcomed. She allows others to navigate their lives.

As an Empress, your energy speaks volumes before you ever utter a word. Imagine yourself right before entering a room. You stand tall, take a deep breath, put a smile on your face, and walk in. Inside, you feel powerful, confident, clever, and filled with regal energy. You can feel this way by changing your energetic sovereign. You change your thoughts and shift your energy through your intention. When you can silence the judgmental voices in your head and instead focus on feeling good about yourself and the goodness in your heart, you can raise your vibration, which in turn raises the vibration of everyone around you. This vibration ripples out into the world creating a global change.

As an Empress, you carry yourself with the quiet confidence of a woman who knows her worth. You may find that people are drawn to you just to be in your presence. They want to be in your energy. This magnetism doesn't come from flashy displays — it emanates from within. It comes from the deep well of self-knowledge and self-acceptance that you've cultivated through your years.

Your energy is a precious commodity. If you waste your time on things that don't serve you, then your energy becomes depleted. When you take care of yourself, focus on a healthy lifestyle, cultivate a social network, act kindly toward others, and invite other positive influences into your life, then your energy becomes enriched. How you live your life affects the quality of your energy.

You choose the way you want to live. You define your own standards of what aging and beauty means to you by questioning and even breaking free from media-driven ideals of physical appearance. You value health and vitality over appearance. There is beauty that goes beyond wearing makeup or being a certain size. Beauty comes from kindness, compassion, authenticity, and feeling confident and self-assured.

Your personal power comes from feeling resourceful and resilient because you have already overcome challenges or moved through transitions in your life. This journey requires not just strength, but also deep self-compassion — honoring your wounds as teachers and treating yourself with the same kindness you'd offer a dear friend. When you embrace your imperfections with gentleness rather than harsh judgement, you transform vulnerability into authentic power. This inner work naturally extends outward, creating space for deeper connections with others.

By embracing others on this journey, you create collaborative approaches instead of competitive ones. You belong to or create communities that uplift you while you elevate others in return. These social networks — whether family, friends, or a tribe of Empresses who gather regularly for tea, a walk, or change-making discussions — form vital circles of wisdom, intuition, experience, and energy. Through these connections, you both receive and give nourishment, choosing to surround yourself with those who celebrate life and add to your spirit essence, not diminish it.

It is important to cultivate relationships with people whose energy resonates with yours or who aspire to cultivate similar vibrations. If you are positive and embrace life in a way that makes you feel alive, then invite the same energy into your circle. If you see someone who is lost on her journey to becoming an Empress, share your wisdom and ask that she consider getting outside help or find resources that can help her rewrite her inner narrative. It's easy to fall prey to negative self-talk or allow others to mentally drain you. If you see a sister or an Empress in need, guide her. If you see that her crown is a bit crooked, help her straighten it out. In this way, we honor the importance of sisterhood, creating a network of Empresses who lift each other toward their highest potential.

As an Empress in your full sovereignty, you have the power to:

- Release outdated patterns and silence negative self-talk. Replace those with empowering beliefs about yourself and how you want to live your life.

- Define your own standards of wellness and beauty by choosing not to succumb to society's constant pursuit of youthful appearance. Instead, honor your body with practices that bring you genuine joy and vitality, whether that's gentle yoga, qigong, vibrant dance, or peaceful walks.

- Rewrite your story without seeking permission from anyone. You have the power to create entirely new experiences. Who says that once you hit a certain age, you can't have new adventures?

- Build communities that celebrate rather than diminish this phase of life. Surrounding yourself with other Empresses who celebrate their lives only enriches yours. Instead of talking about your ailments, talk about what excites you and what you're passionate about. Share or create new rituals, discuss helpful resources, and support each other.

Through your radiant example, you can become an inspiration for younger women, transforming their perception of what later years can be. As they witness your freedom, creativity, and power, they will no longer fear the passage of time but look forward to their own Empress years with excitement.

Remember, dear Empress, that by claiming your crown and redefining this phase of life, you become a beacon of possibility for women everywhere. Each time you stand in your magnificence, you grant permission for others to do the same. Together we form an unbroken circle of Empresses — each sovereign in her own right — yet connected in our collective rising. As we refuse to be diminished, and instead step fully into our power, we don't just change our individual stories, we rewrite the narrative of what it means to be a woman in today's world.

YOUR ROYAL INVITATION

SACRED REFLECTION

Find a quiet moment and comfortable space where you can reflect deeply. Consider the following questions either in meditation or by journaling.

- What societal narratives about aging have you internalized that no longer serve you?
- What wisdom have you gathered that deserves to be honored and shared?
- How would your life change if you fully embraced your power as an Empress?

ROYAL DECLARATION

Create a powerful and personal declaration that helps you embrace your Empress energy. Place it somewhere where you can see it as a reminder of your journey. You can use one of the following or create one of your own.

I am an Empress Rising. I claim my seat on the throne of my own kingdom. I honor the wisdom I've earned through every joy and challenge.

I am not invisible. I am an Empress stepping fully into my power.

I am an Empress — regal, poised, graceful, empowered and empowering.

From this day forward, I embrace my Empress energy. I declare myself sovereign over my life.

CREATE A SACRED CIRCLE

Invite trusted women in your life to gather in a sacred space and share
this book's vision of redefining the "crone years" as "Empress years."
Take turns acknowledging the wisdom, power and radiance you see in
each other. Create small rituals or follow the Royal Invitations in this
book together, experiencing firsthand how one woman claiming her
throne inspires others.

CHAPTER 2

THE EMPRESS'S THRONE: YOUR SACRED SOVEREIGN SPACE

Every Empress deserves a throne. As an Empress, you need both a ceremonial chair or sacred space where you can go to pause, reflect, and gather your thoughts, and an inner sanctuary that travels with you everywhere. Your physical throne serves as a haven where you can take time for yourself, while your inner throne represents your center of personal power. Together, these thrones — one external, one internal — honor your need for personal space.

Throughout your life, you've likely shared your physical space with others and, perhaps given away some of your personal power along the way. Now is the time to reclaim your sovereign space in both realms.

Your Inner Throne

The most powerful throne of all resides within you — the centered place that you can access anytime and anywhere. It travels with you. It's the permission you give yourself to pause and ground yourself amid chaos, knowing you can tap into your intuitive guidance and allow the messages to be received. It's your inner sanctuary where you can observe what is occurring within and around you. It's the inner voice of self-compassion. It's allowing yourself the grace to connect with your emotions and sit with what is showing up for you at any given time. Think of it as your portable palace, always available within yourself.

Your inner throne is accessed through mindful moments such as meditation, walks in nature or sitting on your physical throne or in your sacred space. Journaling can also serve as a gateway especially when you write from a place of deep listening. It's also in those moments that bring you joy such as precious time spent playing with your grandchildren, or when you're having tea with friends and feel a sense of camaraderie. It's the best friend that resides within you, and a treasure chest of experiences that guide your decisions.

Your inner throne is a source of power, wisdom, and refuge. Imagine that your inner throne is a room — a quiet sanctuary where intuition merges with learned wisdom. In this room are shelves filled with books each representing different parts of your life, every page rich with personal history. This is a space you can access anytime and anywhere, where you shed others' expectations and stand in your unwavering truth. It's a space to breathe, center, and ground yourself.

When you regularly connect with your inner throne, you'll notice profound shifts in how you navigate life. Decision-making becomes more aligned with your values rather than external pressures. You may be less swayed by someone else's opinion and more anchored in your own truth. From this center, you can also observe emotions without being overwhelmed by them. Your inner throne gives you direct access to your intuitive guidance — that place that provides answers to your most pressing questions. When you enter a state of solitude and reflection, you are better able to tap into your personal wisdom and allow creative insights and solutions to surface naturally.

As I've stepped into my Empress energy, I find that my inner throne serves as a personal therapist. When I need to reflect on a situation or process an emotional reaction, I retreat to this space where I can explore my feelings with compassion and clarity, free from external judgement or pressure.

My inner throne has become particularly vital since my breast cancer diagnosis. Every year, I undergo regular breast MRIs. After a mastectomy on my right side, I've committed to this yearly screening plan, finding comfort in this routine, while knowing it was an MRI that initially detected the cancer. Living with this history means

I'm always somewhat vigilant, especially during the moments when something suspicious has appeared on the scan, requiring a biopsy.

I imagine many of you have faced similar situations and understand the flood of emotions that surge through your body during these moments of waiting and uncertainty. It's genuinely taxing on the nervous system and utterly exhausting. I consciously retreat to my inner throne — placing my hands over my heart and simply breathe. I give myself permission to feel whatever arises — fear, hope, anger, gratitude — with the compassion I would give to a dear friend. From this centered place, I allow healing wisdom to restore my energy and return me to a more balanced state, allowing me to move through these moments with grace.

The inner throne's power can be enhanced through creating a physical space. While your inner throne travels with you everywhere, a dedicated physical throne in your environment serves as a visible reminder of your commitment to self-care and reflection. It serves as a place to connect to your inner wisdom and nurture the relationship with yourself.

A Physical Throne: Creating Your Sacred Sanctuary

It is equally important to have a physical representation of a throne within your surroundings. It doesn't have to be expensive or elaborate. It can be a special chair, a room, or a sunlit corner adorned with your favorite things. What matters is the intention that you put into this space. It can be a place where you go to make decisions, read a book, or tap into your inner throne.

If men can have "caves," then you can create a special sanctuary where you can be undisturbed and tap into your regal essence. It's not selfish, it's necessary. By honoring yourself you are modeling self-respect and authority. It's important to let others in your environment or household know of your sacred space and establish clear boundaries with them about this place. If it is shared space, you may want to create a schedule that honors your time and ensures that everyone sticks to it. Communicating your needs is important. You are asking others to respect your time and energy, and in so doing, you are prioritizing your own needs.

Your physical throne can look like any of the following:

- A sunlit corner adorned with candles, crystals and oracle cards
- A garden bench surrounded by nature's gifts
- A comfortable chair in your private study
- A meditation cushion in a quiet nook
- A beach chair nearby the ocean
- Your car during moments of solitude

What matters isn't the opulence of the space, but the energy you invest in it. I have an egg-shaped chair suspended in my garden where I retreat when the world becomes too noisy. There, cocooned in comfort, I can disappear into meditation, writing, or music, letting everything else fall away. My family knows that when I'm in this sacred space, I've temporarily stepped into another realm.

In my home, my office serves as my primary throne. This mini kingdom houses treasured artifacts, which include:

- Books and journals filled with wisdom
- Crystals charging the space with energy
- Photos of my children linking past to future
- Feathers and sacred objects
- Statues of saints and deities

This space holds my stories — past, present, and future. It's also where I create, correspond, and commune with my highest self. Every object has been chosen with intention; every element carefully curated to support my Empress energy. This physical sanctuary creates a reminder of my commitment to honor myself.

Regardless of the space you choose to designate as your throne or sacred sanctuary, it requires regular energetic maintenance. Just as dust accumulates naturally in physical spaces, energy often becomes stuck or stagnant over time. You'll recognize this stagnation through subtle signals — your mind becomes foggy, you feel "off" or depleted when you're within that space.

When you notice these signs, it's time for an energetic clearing. Start by opening windows to let fresh air circulate. If you don't have windows, try alternate methods:

- Burn sage or palo santo, using the smoke to purify the space.
- Spray essential oils with clearing properties like lavender, or frankincense.
- Remove any accumulated clutter, which can trap and hold stagnant energy.
- Place clear quarts or selenite crystals in the room, particularly in corners where energy tends to stagnate.
- Use Reiki techniques to clear the space.
- Apply feng shui principles to optimize energy flow throughout your sanctuary.

These simple techniques can become part of a regular routine — what I like to call "regal rituals" — regular practices that honor your sacred space. Your regal rituals might include energy clearing, but they can extend to many other practices that help you feel good. For example, buying yourself flowers weekly can be a beautiful ritual. These small but powerful acts create the message that you are worthy of beauty, attention, and care.

Dear Empress, remember that both your inner and outer thrones are spaces that honor your wisdom, power, and sovereignty. This sacred seat awaits, and it's time for you to claim your rightful place.

YOUR ROYAL INVITATION

As an Empress, you deserve both an inner sanctuary that travels with you everywhere and a physical space that honors your sovereignty. The practices below will help you cultivate and strengthen both your inner throne – that centered place of wisdom and self-compassion – and your outer throne – the physical sanctuary where you can retreat, reflect, and restore your energy. Together, these two thrones form the foundation of your sovereign power, ensuring you always have access to your center, whether you're navigating the world or seeking sacred solitude in your own realm.

CONNECTING WITH YOUR INNER THRONE

Your inner throne is a portable sanctuary of wisdom and peace that you can access anywhere, anytime. These practices will help you strengthen your connection to this sacred center within.

Daily Sacred Pause
Set aside five to ten minutes each day to sit in quiet presence. Close your eyes, place your hands over your heart, and simply breathe. Allow yourself to enter your inner sanctuary where wisdom, compassion, and sovereignty reside.

Access Your Inner Library
Visualize entering the room of your inner throne, with shelves filled with the books of your life experiences. Choose one challenge you've overcome and reflect on the wisdom gained. How might that wisdom serve you now?

Emotional Awareness Practice
When strong emotions arise, mentally step onto your inner throne. From this centered place, observe and feel your emotions without

judgment. Ask yourself: "what triggered this emotion?" "What is this feeling trying to teach me?" "Where do I feel it in my body?" Record your insights in a journal dedicated to your Empress journey.

Self-Compassion Ritual

Create a phrase that represents the voice of your inner throne — words of compassion and kindness you can call upon when needed. For example:

I honor my journey.

I treat myself with the kindness I deserve.

I am enough, exactly as I am

I give myself permission to be imperfect.

I offer myself the same compassion I give to others.

My mistakes do not define my worth.

CREATING YOUR PHYSICAL THRONE

A dedicated physical space serves as a tangible reminder of your commitment to honoring yourself and your sovereignty. These practices will guide you in creating and maintaining a sacred sanctuary in your environment.

Sacred Space

Identify a room or area in your home that will serve as your physical throne. This might be a specific chair, a corner of a room, or an entire space dedicated to your sovereign self. Trust your intuition in making this selection.

Share with those in your household what this space means to you. Establish boundaries by clearly communicating how they can respect your time there. Consider creating a simple signal (like a ribbon on the door knob or "do not disturb' sign) that indicates you are in your sovereign space.

Adornment

Gather three to five objects that represent your Empress energy:

- Something that symbolizes wisdom (perhaps a special book or journal)
- An item that brings comfort (a beautiful cushion or soft throw)
- An object that inspires creativity or joy (artwork, crystals, or photographs)
- A natural element (flowers, plants, feathers, or stones)
- Something that connects you to your spiritual practice (sacred texts or prayer beads)

Space-Clearing Ritual

Establish a weekly ceremony to clear and refresh your throne's energy. This might include:

- Opening windows to allow fresh air to circulate
- Using sage, palo santo, or a selenite wand to clear stagnant energy
- Adding fresh flowers
- Spritzing your favorite essential oil blend

Commit to spending at least fifteen minutes in your throne space three times per week. Use this time to read, journal, meditate, or simply be. Notice how regularly visiting this space transforms your energy and presence in the world.

CHAPTER 3

THE LOTUS CROWN:
THE CONNECTION TO DIVINE POWER

A crown marks sovereignty, but our crown as Empresses is more than mere adornment; it's the seat of our spiritual power. Located at the crown of our head, this energy center serves as our connection to something greater than ourselves, whether we call it the Divine, the Universe, or Spirit.

Through our crown, we are connected to universal life force energy — something bigger than ourselves. When this energy flows freely, we feel guided by Spirit, angels, ancestors, and inner wisdom. We feel held within the larger lens of the cosmic universe. Yet like any precious connection, this link isn't always strong. Life's daily demands and distractions can leave us feeling disconnected and alone, and our energy can become blocked by stress, fear, or everyday concerns.

The lotus represents enlightenment and rebirth. Rising through murky waters to blossom in radiant beauty, it mirrors the journey we take as Empresses. Although we face many challenges and weather transformations, we emerge not despite our struggles, but because of them. This powerful symbol of strength and resilience has become an important part of my own meditation practice, serving as a sacred gateway to the spirit realm — a connection to the Divine.

My own spiritual journey began when I sought deeper connections beyond the physical world. Exploring relationships with spiritual guides brought unexpected comfort during periods of isolation and struggle. This connection reassured me that even in my darkest moments, I was never truly alone.

When I seek guidance and want to connect with Spirit (inner wisdom, archangels, or universal energy in general), I begin by envisioning a large lotus flower at my crown — a living, breathing portal to the Divine. I see myself seated within this sacred bloom, creating space for my guides to join me in counsel. A rainbow light emanates from this lotus, extending upward to connect with universal energy while simultaneously expanding my personal energetic field. My breath serves as an anchor that connects me to both the earth's grounding energy and the spiritual realm. I recognize the connection has been established when I feel a distinctive tingling sensation on my right side accompanied by a sense of peace. I then ask for guidance and open myself to receiving messages.

The lotus is often used to symbolize the crown chakra within our energy system. These energy centers, when properly aligned and flowing, create harmony throughout our physical, emotional, and spiritual bodies. The crown chakra, at the top of our head, serves as a portal to something greater than us. Meanwhile, the root chakra, located at the base of our spine, grounds us to earth's stabilizing energy. Energy flows through us, connecting heaven and earth.

The lotus crown also connects you to a collective consciousness of women who have chosen to live with intention, purpose, and joy. Through this crown, this magnificent lotus of light, you are never truly alone. You are part of an ageless sisterhood of Empresses who support and uplift one another across space and time.

Just as every lotus must grow through murky waters to reach the light, your journey to this sacred sisterhood has been earned through experience. Reflect on the challenges you've faced and overcome. Each difficulty was another layer of murky water your spiritual lotus had to grow through. Now, in your Empress years, you bloom above those waters. This isn't the end of your growth — it's a glorious new beginning of your sovereign chapter.

Your crown, dear Empress, isn't just a symbol; it's a testament to the inner light you've cultivated through decades of experience. Acknowledge the magnificent being you've become, having conquered every challenge and gained wisdom along the way. For every experience, you've earned a gem that rightfully belongs in your beautiful crown. Honor yourself by proudly wearing it, a symbol of your resilience and rich history.

YOUR ROYAL INVITATION

The Lotus Crown Activation is a powerful meditation that helps you connect with divine energy and open your crown chakra—your personal portal to higher guidance. This practice anchors divine light throughout your entire being, strengthening your ability to receive guidance and feel supported by the universal wisdom that flows through all Empresses.

The Lotus Crown Activation

Begin by settling into your sacred space — a quiet room, your physical throne, or simply a few uninterrupted moments that are just for you. You may wish to light a candle.

Close your eyes and take three deep, soul-nourishing breaths.

With each inhale, imagine drawing in golden light that fills every cell of your being.

With each exhale, release any tension, worry, or energy that feels heavy or stagnant.

Feel yourself sinking deeper into this moment, your awareness becoming crystal clear and fully present.

Now, envision a magnificent lotus flower at the crown of your head — its petals a brilliant white with hints of gold, perfectly formed and radiating light.

Notice as each petal slowly unfurls in perfect synchronicity with your breath.

This lotus is your personal gateway to the Divine — the same light that has crowned countless women in their sovereignty.

As the lotus blossoms fully, imagine a warm, radiant light (it can be rainbow light or any color that resonates with your soul) descending gently through its center.

Feel this light enter through your crown chakra, like warm honey flowing gently downward. Take a moment to breathe with this divine energy as it begins to fill your being.

Gently flowing down through your head, illuminating your mind with clarity and wisdom. Pause here and feel this light settling into your thoughts.

Warming your throat and empowering your voice to speak your truth with confidence and grace.

Expanding your heart space, filling it with unconditional love and deep compassion for yourself and others.

Flowing into your solar plexus, igniting your personal power like a golden flame within.

Settling in your sacral center, awakening your creativity and passion.

Moving to the base of your spine, rooting you in strength and stability and connecting you deeply to Mother Earth's supportive embrace.

Allow three natural breaths as this energy settles completely within you.

Feel your entire being now glow with radiance — each cell awakened, alive with sacred light.

In this luminous state, feel yourself connecting with the universal divine feminine energy.

Sense the presence of Empresses across time and space — women of wisdom, strength, and grace who have walked this path before you and those who walk it alongside you now.

Feel their ancient wisdom flowing toward you, their loving presence surrounding you like a protective, radiant embrace.

Visualize golden threads of light extending from your crown, weaving out to connect with other light-bearers around the globe.

You are part of an infinite web of divine feminine wisdom.

As you rise, you help others rise.

As you shine, you illuminate the path for others.

As you remember who you are, you call others home to themselves.

Take a moment to feel the power of this connection. Let it fill you with certainty and peace.

This is the true purpose of your crown — not to set you apart, but to help you connect more deeply with yourself, Spirit, and the sacred sisterhood of all beings.

When you're ready, slowly bring your awareness back to your body and physical space.

Feel your feet rooted on the earth.

Place your hands over your heart, anchoring this radiant energy within you.

The light and connections remain with you, woven into your very essence.

Know that this lotus crown stays with you always — a living reminder of your divine connection, your power, and your place in the sacred circle of Empresses.

Place your hands over your heart once more and offer a gentle bow — in gratitude, in reverence, in love.

Carry this radiance with you as you move through your day, knowing you are both supported and supporting, both teaching and learning, both growing and whole. Return to this meditation whenever you need to remember your light, your connection, your crown.

The lotus is always within you — waiting to bloom again and again.

CHAPTER 4

SELF-MASTERY: CRAFTING YOUR LIFE WITH INTENTION AND AWARENESS

Self-mastery and self-sovereignty are two vital aspects of embodying Empress energy. Each playing a distinct yet complementary role in your growth and evolution. Self-mastery is gaining an understanding of yourself — your emotions, your strengths, and even your limitations. It's recognizing the lessons you've learned and the tools that help you navigate your experiences. It also means showing yourself compassion when you have faltered or been hurt, and standing firm when you need to guard your energy. These elements form the unshakeable pillars upon which your kingdom is built.

Think of self-mastery as learning to skillfully pilot a ship, while self-sovereignty is recognizing that you are the rightful captain of that ship, with the authority to chart your own course. You've weathered storms, navigated treacherous waters, and learned from every voyage. Now you've have earned the right to sit in the captain's chair — or in your case, the Empress throne.

Your life is a continuous journey of learning and personal development. You have a wealth of resources that can help nurture your mind, body, and spirit when you feel out of balance. Self-help books, experts in various fields from health to relationships, meditations, and movement practices can all assist you. When you embody the Empress energy, you are recognizing that you are a work of art but still a work in progress. You have the freedom to be your own teacher, healer, and guide, but you also have the option to seek guidance when needed.

Self-mastery involves developing skills and gaining awareness over different aspects of your life. When I began a regular yoga practice during a time when I felt spiritually broken and in chronic pain, I began to reconnect to myself and unpack what was happening emotionally. This practice helped me rediscover my internal guidance system. I realized how effective this practice was in helping me understand what was happening both physically and emotionally. Through self-observation, I learned to recognize when something felt out of balance and what I needed to support my healing journey. Through consistent awareness, I learned to interpret my emotions, energy, thoughts, and actions. I also incorporated other practices like qigong, meditation, new and full moon rituals, and Reiki into my routine. I have discovered what works for me, and it's important for you to learn what helps you. What are some practices that you have nurtured that are readily available when needed.

Several years ago, I began evaluating my relationship with alcohol — a relationship that had spanned decades. This reflection sparked a deep awareness of how alcohol affected me both physically and emotionally. The morning after drinking, I'd feel awful: my mind foggy, my skin puffy, my energy diminished. More than the physical effects, I noticed how it impacted my self-esteem. I'd engage in negative self-talk, berating myself for drinking the night before, feeling as though it was dimming my light and pulling me away from my authentic self.

This growing awareness forced me to confront the deeper roots of this pattern. I had grown up in a family where wine was served nightly, which normalized alcohol in daily life. My own drinking began in my teenage years when peer pressure drew me to partying as a way to fit in and make friends. This pattern of social drinking simply continued into adulthood.

Since becoming an energy worker and especially after my cancer diagnosis, my relationship with alcohol shifted dramatically. I learned that it could increase inflammation in the body, and after my father passed away from cancer linked to drinking and smoking, the awareness became even more acute. Though I'd stopped during pregnancy and never drank daily, I knew deep down that any amount of alcohol wasn't serving my highest good.

As I paid closer attention to my body's responses, the effects became increasingly clear: disturbed sleep patterns, night sweats, gut issues, and brain fog. Sometimes drinking would lead to unnecessary relationship friction — fights or words that wouldn't have been expressed otherwise. As an Empress, I realized this pattern wasn't aligned with who I was becoming.

My journey to freedom from alcohol combined practical steps with spiritual practices. I began incorporating these specific exercises:

- Daily journaling, especially during full moons, to release what no longer served me

- Morning and evening Reiki self-treatments

- Qigong practices with specific movements intended to shift deep-rooted energy patterns

- Calling on spiritual support from my guides and archangels, especially Raphael for healing and Michael for protection

I also had to identify and address my triggers. Cooking dinner had been a cue to pour a glass of wine, as had coming home after a stressful day. Social situations presented the biggest challenge. I worried about what others would think if I wasn't holding a cocktail in my hand. But embodying Empress energy meant releasing the need for others' approval. I learned to simply state that I wasn't drinking anymore, and people respected my choice.

The path to becoming alcohol-free wasn't easy. It required facing physical withdrawals, navigating social situations, and reprogramming longstanding habits. I replaced the cocktail or wine with iced tea or juice in a fancy glass and educated myself about alcohol's effects on the body and brain. This education allowed me to challenge the media portrayal of alcohol as a necessary ingredient for a fun, sophisticated life.

The benefits of this transformation have been profound. I sleep better without night sweats because my body is no longer working overtime processing toxins. I have improved mental clarity, and I feel more genuinely myself. I am also a clearer channel when doing Reiki healing on myself and others and my intuition is stronger. This journey exemplified both self-mastery and self-sovereignty. The self-mastery came through the disciplined work of changing a pattern, while self-sovereignty emerged as I claimed my right to make choices that serve my highest good, regardless of social norms.

While this is my personal story and not a prescription for others, it demonstrates how awareness, intention, and consistent practice can transform deeply ingrained patterns. When I realized that alcohol wasn't necessary in my life and was negatively impacting my health and inner peace, it became easier for me to let go of it.

As an Empress, you have the power to recognize what doesn't serve you and the sovereignty to choose a different path. Self-awareness is the cornerstone of self-mastery, acting as both the compass and the map on your journey to personal sovereignty. For an Empress, self-awareness goes beyond simple self-observation — it's a deep and honest recognition of your energy, patterns, triggers, strengths, and areas for growth.

On the physical level, it means understanding your body's signals and rhythms — knowing when you need rest, movement, or nourishment. On the emotional level, it helps you understand your triggers and navigate moments with grace, self-compassion, and wisdom. More importantly, self-awareness helps you to recognize the difference between conditioned responses and authentic choices. It helps you to recognize when you own your power versus when you give it away. Before you can transform any pattern, you must be aware of it — recognizing both your capabilities and your limitations.

The journey to self-mastery requires an ongoing commitment to self-awareness — a willingness to look honestly at yourself without judgment and criticism while maintaining the dignity and compassion befitting an Empress. Change is continuous. You are not the same person you were three years ago or even a few months ago, and you will be a different person in the future. Discover and embrace new ways to create a life that embodies your deepest values and celebrates your evolution.

YOUR ROYAL INVITATION

Self-Mastery is about exploring and applying practical techniques that enhance your awareness. These tools — such as meditation, mindful movement, journaling, breathwork, and energy practices — can become part of your daily routine. While you may already incorporate some of these practices, I encourage you to remain curious and explore new modalities. Take inventory of what you currently practice and consider adding something new, perhaps a movement practice like qigong or yoga. Even if you believe you're not flexible enough for yoga, gentler forms like Hatha, or yin yoga, can be accessible to most. Qigong offers another option that cultivates a healthier flow of energy while developing your ability to sense and work with the different qualities of your energetic state.

As you build your self-mastery toolkit, consider balance by including activities that nurture your physical body through movement, feed your spirit through contemplative practices and stimulate your mind through learning. Keep an open mind and have fun. Exploring new things is like window shopping, where you browse until something catches your eye. If a practice resonates with you, keep it in your toolkit; if it doesn't, put it back on the shelf.

As an Empress, you will invite in what feels right. You may discover that when you start integrating something new and different, you naturally eliminate what no longer serves you. Every change shifts your energy, which is why when you do things that align with your deepest values and vision for your life, you make them part of your regular practice.

Here are some self-mastery practices to consider:

- Begin a daily movement practice, like qigong or yoga, even if just for ten minutes.
- Focus on proper posture and alignment. Practice standing tall with shoulders back and head high

- Create a morning routine that energizes you
- Learn to recognize your energy peaks and valleys
- Schedule activities according to your natural rhythms
- Practice deep breathing exercises
- Maintain regular sleep patterns
- Create an organized, peaceful living space
- Establish a sacred corner or room for practice (your throne)
- Keep a daily journal that helps you track emotional patterns and triggers
- Practice naming emotions as they arise
- Notice physical sensations linked to emotions
- Develop awareness of emotional weather patterns
- Honor your own needs first
- Observe your thoughts without attachment
- Challenge negative self-talk
- Develop positive thought patterns
- Read regularly in areas of interest
- Take courses in new subjects
- Learn from younger generations
- Stay current with technology
- Embrace beginner's mind
- Connect with nature regularly
- Practice gratitude
- Cultivate inner silence

Remember that self-mastery is a journey, not a destination. Progress comes through consistent practice and patient persistence. Each small step forward builds upon the last, creating a foundation for continued growth and development.

CHAPTER 5

SELF–SOVEREIGNTY:
THE COURAGE TO LIVE
ON YOUR OWN TERMS

Self-sovereignty is claiming and exercising authority over your life. It is not something that you need to learn or develop; it is your birthright. Self-sovereignty is about recognizing and claiming your right to set boundaries and make decisions aligned with your values with no need for external validation. It's about recognizing your inherent worth and using your power with wisdom and purpose. As you step through the gateway to your personal kingdom, you'll find that everything you need already resides within you.

True sovereignty comes from being both empowered and responsible. An Empress doesn't blame others or play the victim when things go wrong. Instead, she takes ownership of her choices and actions, knowing that her experiences have taught her what works and what doesn't.

This doesn't mean she's hard on herself when she stumbles or makes mistakes. Self-sovereignty includes self-compassion – recognizing that being human means being imperfect and that wisdom often comes through the very experiences we wish we could change.

We often say, "If I only knew then what I know now." But an Empress understands that those lessons were necessary steps on her journey. Now, armed with this wisdom, you can make choices that align with your values and authentically express your power.

Self-sovereignty also means trusting your inner compass over external expectations. When society, family, or even well-meaning friends suggest what you 'should do', an Empress pauses, goes to her inner throne, and asks: "What feels true for me?" She honors both her intuitive wisdom and her hard-earned life experience when making decisions.

Having Energetic Boundaries

Let me tell you about a client I'll call Sally whose story illustrates the importance of energetic boundaries. Sally's serene nature and listening skills made her a magnet for others, particularly one friend who would call every morning to unleash a torrent of complaints and frustrations. These one-sided conversations drained Sally's energy, yet she struggled to set boundaries.

When Sally began attending morning fitness classes that occurred during these traditional call times, she discovered something remarkable: She felt energized rather than depleted, surrounded by positive energy instead of negativity. Though Sally's friend initially chose to stop communicating with her abruptly after Sally began devoting more time to her personal practice and less on lending an ear to her friend's rants, they eventually rebuilt their relationship on more balanced terms. This wasn't just about ending a toxic pattern; it was about Sally claiming her control over her time and energy and learning to create energetic boundaries.

Sally's story illustrates a crucial principle: energetic boundaries often require practical changes, not just internal shifts. Sometimes we think we can simply 'think' our way to better boundaries, but true sovereignty often demands concrete action. Sally didn't just visualize protection from her friend's negativity — she literally changed her availability. An Empress understands that energetic boundaries and practical boundaries work hand in hand.

This experience taught Sally — and teaches all of us — that setting energetic boundaries isn't about rejecting people or being unkind. It's about honoring your own energy as the precious resource it is. When Sally protected her morning energy, she wasn't punishing her friend; she was preserving her capacity to show up fully in all areas of her life. A depleted Empress serves no one well, but a nourished Empress can offer her gifts from a place of abundance rather than obligation.

Writing Your Own Story

One of the most powerful expressions of self-sovereignty is claiming authorship of your own life story. Yet many of us have chapters where we allowed others to hold the pen, letting their fears, limitations, or expectations shape our narrative. In my early teens, I dreamed of becoming a sports journalist. I wrote for the school and local papers and set my heart on studying journalism. Then someone close to me suggested this career would be "too challenging for a woman" in an era when female journalists were scarce, and I allowed their words to override my dream. Without the self-confidence I now possess, I let others' limitations become my own.

Though my path led me to different forms of expression — writing, podcasting, teaching — this experience taught me a valuable lesson about sovereignty: Only you can write the story of your life. Others may offer suggestions or advice, but an Empress knows she is the ultimate authority in her kingdom. This authority extends to every choice you make — from career decisions to relationships, from how you spend your time to how you respond to challenges.

Self-sovereignty requires energetic integrity — the alignment of your thoughts, words, and actions with your authentic self. This means making decisions based on your values, not others' expectations. It's about speaking your truth with grace and conviction, even when it's uncomfortable. An Empress protects her energy while remaining open to genuine connections, respecting her personal boundaries and those she encounters. She recognizes when to extend her energy toward others and when to conserve it for herself, honoring her own needs.

Through this energetic integrity, she creates the chapters of her own life. But learning to honor our own needs while respecting others is a skill that develops over time. How often do we make decisions based on what we believe will make someone else happy or benefit them. We've all done it. We choose to agree with someone else's decision because it's easier or because we feel that our own desires don't matter. Looking back at my own relationships, I can see how often I fell into this pattern, especially in the early stages when I wanted to be agreeable and accommodating.

When I first started dating my husband, Brian, I decided to take up skiing because it was something he enjoyed. It was terrifying; at thirty-six, I'd never worn skis before. During a ski weekend at Killington, Vermont, I took lessons and managed the beginner slopes. Despite more lessons on subsequent trips, I never felt comfortable skiing. When we got engaged and planned our honeymoon, Brian suggested Whistler in British Columbia — a skier's paradise that I found intimidating. I agreed because I knew he was an active outdoorsman, though I would have preferred slipping on flip flops and walking tropical beaches somewhere warm.

Years later I admitted to Brian that Whistler wasn't my honeymoon of choice. What kept me from stating my truth? Perhaps I felt that my opinion wasn't valuable or that his preferences should take priority over mine. I've since learned to be more direct and honest, not just when planning vacations but in all areas of our relationship, recognizing that my voice and desires are equally important in creating a balanced partnership.

Your voice is important, and a vital aspect lies in expressing what truly matters to you. While you deserve to be heard, the art lies in how you communicate your truth. Frame your thoughts carefully and choose your words with intention, speaking with both clarity and compassion. This sovereignty extends to honoring others' voices with the same courtesy, creating space for their perspectives even when you disagree. The Empress understands that speaking her truth and listening deeply are equally sacred practices.

Active listening is a phrase commonly used today. In a world of countless distractions, we are losing our ability to listen. Active listening is the same as listening mindfully — being in the present moment and hearing what another person is saying. Have you ever started talking and the person looks down at their phone and starts scrolling. It's rude, right? Does that annoy you? Or do you shrug it off as a normal occurrence? Do you find yourself doing it mindlessly looking at your phone when someone else is talking to you? If so, please stop and practice active listening.

Be an example for someone else so when the person you're talking to looks down at their phone, you can kindly say something like, "Excuse me, would you mind not looking at your phone while I speak to you?" You state it simply and graciously, clearly communicating that you value being heard.

Expressing your truth often requires walking a fine line. You may feel the need to say something but then realize that it may hurt someone's feelings. Frame your thoughts first then carefully choose your words before voicing them. If telling someone that their breath needs refreshing might upset them, perhaps simply offer them mints instead. Sometimes compassionate boundaries involve choosing when and how to communicate difficult truths.

Sometimes boundaries aren't just about what you say, they're also about recognizing when to step back to protect your own well-being. Learning to pause before reacting to triggering conversations gives you space to respond from your centered self rather than emotional reactivity. It's okay to withdraw from conversations or activities that could drain you physically or emotionally without guilt or explanation. Becoming aware of this allows you to restore balance and a harmonious flow of energy when you're feeling imbalanced. Practices like retreating to your physical throne for quiet reflection, qigong, going for a walk, or even taking a nap can help restore your nervous system. Remember, you have the power to replenish yourself when you're feeling depleted.

Remember, your sovereignty isn't about building walls, it's about knowing who you are and honoring that truth in every choice you make. This means saying yes to what aligns with your values and gracefully declining what doesn't, speaking your truth even when it's uncomfortable, and choosing relationships that celebrate rather than diminish your light. Your kingdom flourishes when you rule from a place of authentic power and clear intention.

Can you recall a time in your life when you tried to express your concerns over a situation that would directly affect you only to be dismissed? Or a time when you allowed someone else to make decisions for you because you didn't feel confident or worthy enough to have a say? Consider how frequently you've apologized unnecessarily. We all have said "I'm sorry" far more times than we realize; for many of us it's a phrase on automatic pilot. No matter what happens, we take responsibility and are sorry for it. Challenge yourself to notice when you automatically apologize and reserve those words for moments when it's truly warranted.

Almost every woman I've worked with energetically, through Reiki sessions, comes to me with stagnant energy in their throat and heart chakras. This stagnation occurs when we fail to set boundaries or express our thoughts and feelings. As a result, the energy in our bodies doesn't flow freely, and we eventually feel the consequences, such as thyroid issues, sore throats, and even losing our voices.

It may not always be easy to express what you really want to say or feel, but you can try. Even if you experience pushback from others, as an Empress, you must speak your truth. This may not guarantee that you will be heard, or others will honor your opinion, but at least you can be sovereign in your expression. Of course, there may be times when it's best to refrain from saying anything. By pausing before speaking, going within and asking for guidance, and then listening for the answers, you will know what to do. Trust your own inner wisdom.

As an Empress, you have the power to:

- Set clear boundaries without apology
- Make choices that honor your wisdom and values
- Share your gifts on your own terms
- Create space for what truly matters to you
- Step away from relationships and situations that drain your energy

These sovereign powers form the foundation of your reign. When you embrace these abilities fully, you step into the authentic authority that has always been yours.

YOUR ROYAL INVITATION

To further cultivate this authority in your life, I invite you to explore the following reflections and practices that will strengthen your connection to your inner guidance.

SACRED REFLECTION

Find a quiet space, perhaps your throne, and settle into your power. Place your hands over your heart and take three deep breaths. This will help settle and ground your energy.

When you're ready, ask yourself the following questions. If you'd like, you can write down the answers in your Empress journal.

What areas of your kingdom need stronger boundaries?

Where have you given away power that you'd like to reclaim?

What decisions have you been postponing out of fear of others' opinions?

What truth have you been holding back that needs to be expressed?

TAKING SOVEREIGN ACTION

Choose one area where you'll assert your sovereignty this week. Here are some possibilities that may benefit you:

- Setting a boundary with someone who drains your energy
- Saying no to a commitment that doesn't align with your values
- Making a decision you've been avoiding
- Speaking your truth in a situation that matters to you

Daily Sovereignty Practice
Each morning, place your hand over your heart and declare: "I am the sovereign ruler of my life. Today I choose what serves my highest good."

CHAPTER 6

THE EMBODIED SELF:
ALIGNING BODY, MIND, AND SPIRIT

Our bodies are the kingdom we live in throughout our journey. This physical vessel is the primary space that belongs completely to us — where our spirit dwells and through which we experience everything life offers. Like any home, it requires attentive care, respect, and thoughtful maintenance to function well.

As women in our wisdom years, we understand that our physical bodies carry the beautiful marks of our experiences, storing memories not just in our minds, but in our very tissues, bones, and how we hold ourselves. This lived experience shows visibly in our posture — how we physically present ourselves to the world.

The story of our journey can be read in how we stand, sit, and walk. Years spent caring for others, working at desk jobs, or on our feet, and facing physical challenges have all influenced our physical form. Just as important, our emotions have shaped how we hold ourselves — our bodies often remembering what our minds might forget. Awareness of our physical posture and emotional state gives us a powerful opportunity for positive change as we embrace this stage of life.

Take a moment now to explore your own posture. Whether standing or sitting, gently bring awareness to your spine. As you straighten your back, notice how this simple adjustment creates an immediate shift in your presence. Draw a deep breath into this new alignment. Feel how your chest naturally expands, how the crown of your head lifts toward the sky like a lotus reaching for sunlight. You might discover yourself feeling not just taller, but more present and more grounded in your sovereignty.

The traditional imagery of a crone often portrays an aging woman hunched over, her spine curved by the weight of years and responsibilities. However, that doesn't have to be your destiny! You can have a different physical presence. Through conscious awareness and deliberate practice, you can maintain — or improve — your alignment. When you allow your posture to collapse, rounding your shoulders forward, you create a cascade of physical effects. The front of your body compresses, particularly affecting your heart and lungs. Over time, this compression becomes your body's default pattern, as connective tissue adapts to this shortened position.

Your neck — the cervical spine — bears witness to modern habits. The countless hours spent looking down at devices can lead to chronic tension, headaches, and restricted movement. While these patterns may feel deeply ingrained, it's never too late to invite positive change. As both a yoga and qigong instructor, I've witnessed remarkable transformations through dedicated practice. The body possesses an extraordinary capacity for renewal when you offer it the right support and attention.

The key lies in understanding that posture is not about rigid perfection but about creating space for vitality to flow. Each small adjustment, each moment of postural awareness, contributes to your overall wellbeing. Through mindful movement practices, you can enhance both mobility and flexibility, particularly in the spine — your central channel of life force energy.

Yet the benefits of proper alignment extend far beyond the physical realm. The relationship between posture and emotional well-being runs deeper than mere appearance. Traditional Chinese Medicine illustrates this connection through its understanding of the way emotions reside within your physical organs, creating a map of your emotional and physical landscape.

Each organ system in Traditional Chinese Medicine holds and processes specific emotional energies:

- The heart embraces the spectrum from joy to sadness.
- The liver balances anger with faith.

- The lungs transform grief into acceptance.

- The kidneys transmute fear into courage.

- The stomach shifts worry into calm.

Your body instinctively responds to emotional states through subtle changes in your posture. Consider how you physically protect your heart and lungs during times of profound grief or sadness. Your shoulders naturally draw forward, creating a protective shield around these vital organs. While this instinct serves an immediate purpose, prolonged protective posturing can lead to emotional and energetic stagnation, potentially creating imbalances in your body's energy flow and emotional processing.

This protective response extends beyond grief to any overwhelming emotional experience. Whether you're processing disappointment, fear, anger, or trauma, your body may adopt similar defensive postures. When you lose someone you love, your body may maintain this protective posture, unconsciously holding onto the grief as a final connection to your loved one. Similarly, after experiencing betrayal, your shoulders might remain hunched as if still guarding against future hurt. Or following a period of intense stress, your chest might stay contracted long after the crisis has passed.

Though this response is natural and understandable, it can impede your healing journey. The forward-drawn shoulders that once protected you can become a physical barrier to processing your emotions, particularly affecting the lungs' ability to process grief and the heart's capacity to embrace joy. When you stand tall, you create space for your vital organs to perform optimally. The heart space opens and the lungs expand more freely, receiving the space they need to perform their essential functions.

Your spine serves as a central channel or pathway for your body's vital energy. When you maintain proper posture — shoulders back, spine straight, head aligned — you create optimal conditions for emotional energy to flow freely through your chakras and meridian channels. This alignment isn't just physical; it's an invitation for emotional release and renewal. Think of your posture as a physical expression of emotional courage. When we stand or sit with our spine aligned, we're not just improving our physical health, we're creating space for emotional healing. This upright posture sends a powerful message to your nervous system that it's safe to release protective patterns and allow natural healing to occur.

As you work with posture, remember that the goal isn't to force emotional release but to create the proper conditions for natural healing. When you align your spine and open your heart space, you're essentially signaling to your body that it's safe to process and release stored emotions while also creating space to invite in joy and other uplifting emotions. This physical openness supports the unimpeded flow of energy through your organs, chakras, and meridian systems, allowing emotional healing to unfold at its own perfect rhythm. The Empress understands that the body's wisdom works best when given space and permission to heal naturally.

Energy centers, called chakras, run along the spine, which acts as a conduit of energy. The energy centers are represented as "wheels" that ideally spin freely, allowing life force energy to flow throughout your being. When energy becomes stagnant in the body, the wheels struggle to rotate properly — affecting you both physically and emotionally — similar to how meridians function in Traditional Chinese Medicine. For example, when your root chakra, which is located at the base of the spine, is restricted, you may feel discomfort in your lower body while emotionally feeling ungrounded or unsafe in your environment. Understanding these energy centers helps you maintain sovereignty over your physical and emotional well-being.

These energy centers are connected to different emotions and parts of the body:

- At your foundation lies the root chakra, grounding you in stability and security. When this energy flows freely, you feel safe in your environment and confident in your ability to meet life's basic needs, free from constant fears about survival.

- Just below the navel resides the sacral chakra, which governs your connections with others. This center channels your creative, sensual, and relational energy, inspiring artistic pursuits and influencing your relationships with partners and friends.

- Above it, the solar plexus chakra serves as your power center, where you cultivate self-worth and personal strength. When balanced, it empowers you to make choices aligned with your authentic self. However, when disrupted, you may struggle with boundaries and self-valuation.

- The heart chakra bridges your physical and spiritual energies, nurturing both self-love and your capacity for compassion and unconditional love. This center teaches you that love is the foundation for all healing and transformation.

- Rising to the throat chakra — your center of expression — is where you voice your truth, articulate your needs, and share your deepest dreams and desires.

- The third eye chakra — located at the center of the forehead — expands your perception beyond the physical realm, offering clarity and insight while awakening your intuitive abilities and clairvoyant perception.

- Finally, at the crown chakra, you connect to something greater than yourself. This highest energy center opens us to the Divine, whether you perceive it as Spirit, God, or Universal Consciousness, completing your energetic alignment from Earth to Heaven. This is your Lotus crown.

In my Reiki practice, I've noticed some consistent patterns, particularly among women. The throat, heart, and solar plexus chakras are often the most blocked or stagnant areas I encounter when doing a healing session. When the throat and heart chakras are blocked, clients typically struggle with self-expression, feeling unheard, or experiencing disconnection from their emotions, especially around love and acceptance.

I've worked with countless women who struggle with self-worth, finding themselves unable to make career changes or life transitions with the confidence they deserve. Many remain in situations simply because they believe it's expected of them, gradually silencing their sovereign inner voice until they become trapped in a cycle of self-doubt. These patterns frequently trace back to formative experiences — moments when their unique gifts went unacknowledged, or their authentic expression was discouraged. The journey to reclaiming one's Empress energy begins with recognizing these learned patterns for what they are: not truths, but stories that can be rewritten.

The solar plexus chakra, located at the center of your personal power, plays a crucial role in your sense of confidence and intuitive guidance — that gut feeling that whispers wisdom when you pause to listen. When energy stagnates in this area, it often manifests as feelings of powerlessness and unworthiness, commonly presenting as imposter syndrome – that persistent inner voice that tells you you're not qualified or deserving of your accomplishments, even when you clearly are. I experienced this firsthand when I became a yoga teacher at the age of fifty-five.

Despite over two hundred hours of training and over twenty-five years of practice, I questioned whether I was ready to teach. I had to do the deep inner work to discover what truly caused these doubts. What helped me push through was remembering advice from my early days as a technology trainer: "Rose, you've got this. You're ready. You know more than you think." This reminder became my mantra, helping me realize that growth comes from taking action. If I wanted to be a teacher, I had to start teaching. What I ultimately discovered was that unblocking this energy center allowed me to step into my authentic power and share wisdom that could only come from decades of lived experience.

I learned to welcome feedback and trust that the yoga community would be compassionate if I stumbled. Today, I still feel excited but nervous before teaching, but it's balanced with confidence in my ability to share something I'm deeply passionate about. This journey has shown me how working through energy blocks can transform self-doubt into self-assurance.

There are several techniques you can use to move stagnant energy in the body. Reiki is one powerful method. If you're a Reiki practitioner, you can perform self-Reiki. If you're not trained in Reiki, movement practices like yoga, qigong, and even dancing are excellent alternatives for encouraging energy flow.

Qigong is particularly effective for energy work, as the name itself reveals: qi means energy and gong means skill or work. Qigong combines movement, breath, and intention to cultivate greater awareness and flow of healthy energy throughout the body.

Dancing offers another joyful way to move stagnant energy. Dancing doesn't have to be saved for a special occasion, a partner, or even proper techniques – just put on music that moves you and let your body respond freely. We all have those days when we feel lethargic, sad, or stuck in a funk. When that happens, just put some music on and dance!

In my early thirties, I was in a challenging and emotionally abusive relationship and my physical health was affected. I was experiencing severe joint pain. Various tests were performed but a definitive diagnosis wasn't made. I went to several different doctors who didn't know what was wrong with me. It was a mystery to them. I was told to take pain medication and live with it.

I felt intuitively guided to try yoga. During the early 1990s, there weren't many places near me that offered yoga. We didn't have the Internet, which now allows us to search for "yoga near me." I came across a holistic magazine featuring local practitioners and vendors. In it, I saw a tiny ad about a Hatha yoga class. I didn't know what Hatha was, but something inside me felt drawn to try the class. I wasn't sure if I would be able to do the poses or movements with the discomfort that I was experiencing, but my inner guidance told me that I had to take the class. I wasn't going to settle for living with this pain the rest of my life. I had a feeling that yoga was going to help me heal.

I had no idea what to expect. The class took place in a church's auditorium, chairs pushed aside, spare yoga mats and blocks in a corner. I was greeted by a woman with red hair, white flowy pants, a loose white top, and a big smile. "Hi, my name is Yvette. Welcome!" she said. All I could see was a beautiful being of light and any concern or nervousness that I had simply melted away. I felt at home and at peace in this space. I explained to Yvette what I was physically experiencing and that I had never taken yoga before. She assured me that we would be doing gentle movements and that I could just do what I can. "In this class," she said, "we never compare or compete." That phrase became a personal mantra and one I share with my own students.

I grabbed a yoga mat, blanket, and some blocks and found a space on the floor. There were about five others that evening, and they greeted me with their welcoming smiles. At thirty-one years old, I was the youngest person there, ready to learn from those who had been walking this path longer than me.

Hatha yoga consists of gentle movements with emphasis on awareness of what is occurring in the body as well as the mind. We began every class with breath work and simple seated stretching. Yvette would share personal stories about how simple movements can create lasting change. From seated postures we transitioned to a series of standing ones. Eventually, I was able to move through them with little discomfort. I think that the peaceful environment, a new practice, and my intention to feel better created a wonderful first experience. I decided to make it a regular part of my routine and looked forward to attending my weekly yoga class.

I learned more than just yoga in those classes. Yvette would educate us about the benefits of Ayurvedic medicine and demonstrate the use of a neti pot to clear out your sinuses. This is where I first learned about the chakras. I was learning so much and enjoying every minute of it, while also discovering what it was like to have a weekly self-care routine. I felt at home in this space with my teacher and the other yogis. Yvette taught us to believe in ourselves and that we had the strength to overcome anything. I believe that the spiritual lessons that I learned in class were just as, if not more, important than the physical postures.

The pain in my joints began subsiding with each class and eventually disappeared completely. I felt stronger physically, emotionally, and spiritually because of my yoga practice. I felt more comfortable and in rhythm with my own body, mind, and spirit. I was more aware that I needed to make changes or chart a new path along my journey of transformation. With this stronger body and valued presence, I left the toxic relationship that I was in. That became a pivotal moment in my life and set a course that would lead me here.

I believe the pain that I had been experiencing manifested due to issues within my romantic relationship and the unprocessed grief around the passing of my mom. My mother passed away when I was twenty-six (she was forty-nine). She'd had breast cancer eight years prior, which went into remission until it resurfaced as bone cancer that she eventually died from. I don't think that I fully or properly grieved her loss after she passed. Instead, I distracted myself with work, became involved in unhealthy relationships, worked two jobs, and returned to college to complete my bachelor's degree. The heartache was still there just underneath the surface, but I told myself that I would be okay as long as I kept busy and ignored the pain.

But emotions have a way of rising to the surface. By refusing to address my grief, I was giving it more power over me. Slowly and steadily, it affected my body. I began losing my ability to stand and walk without pain, and just as significantly, I lost my inner strength to walk away from relationships that were harming me. I was hurt and angry and felt abandoned on so many levels. By not taking the time to heal myself and, instead, throwing myself into an unhealthy relationship, I left myself vulnerable and became trapped in a cycle of emotional abuse.

This painful experience taught me a crucial lesson about the mind-body connection that I now share with every woman I work with. It is important to become aware of the signals from your body and your emotions. When you hold onto negative emotions for a long time, they will manifest in your body. Instead, try and recognize when your emotions are surfacing and allow yourself to compassionately work through them. If you repress them, your body will respond. You may get incessant stomach issues or debilitating migraines. You may have physical tension in your back and shoulders, or you might experience emotional ailments such as anxiety, depression, frustration or unexplained fatigue. Whatever surfaces in your body or mind, view it as an invitation to explore what you're truly trying to process in your life.

Doing yoga and discovering a spiritual practice helped me to uncover shadows within my own personality and life that went far beyond grief. The more I learned the tools, the stronger I felt. I gained more confidence in setting boundaries and even leaving relationships that didn't serve a purpose in my life. In a way, I felt that I released a heavy vest from my chest and back, and I finally felt that I was moving in a better direction. I literally felt taller, more self-assured, and more in alignment with my true purpose. I began thinking about what I needed to do for myself instead of what I could do for others. I was able to stand on my own two feet and support myself spiritually and financially.

My journey of self-mastery began in the yoga studio, where both physical and metaphysical practices laid the groundwork for my personal transformation. What started as an intention to heal my body blossomed as the universe provided the perfect environment for growth as I learned to trust my inner guidance. Through this practice, I discovered how to align my energy flow, allowing me to not only glimpse my true essence but also embrace the fulfilling life I was meant to live.

As you tend to your embodied self, remember that how you carry yourself affects not just your physical well-being but your entire energetic presence. Dear Empress, your body is the kingdom where your spirit dwells. Stand tall, lift your crown toward the sky, and honor both the physical vessel that has carried you through your journey and the wisdom you've gained along the way.

YOUR ROYAL INVITATION

This practice integrates the key themes of embodied sovereignty we've explored throughout this chapter. By consciously connecting your physical body with your energetic presence, you'll experience what it truly means to be grounded in your power while open to divine guidance. The following exercise helps you feel supported by the earth and connected to the heavens through your Lotus crown.

Breathing between Heaven and Earth

When you stand tall, you become a living bridge between earth and sky. Take a moment to practice this powerful alignment that connects you to both grounding and divine energies:

1. Stand with your feet hip-width apart, knees slightly bent, arms resting naturally at your sides and spine elongated. Feel the ground beneath you. This is your foundation, supporting you completely.

2. Bring your awareness first to your feet. Feel your connection to the earth, drawing its stabilizing energy upward through your legs and to your root chakra, located at the base of your spine. This energy roots you firmly in place and offers strength and stability.

3. Now shift your awareness to the crown of your head. Feel this area opening like a lotus flower to receive light and wisdom from above — your connection to Spirit, Source, the Divine.

4. As you breathe deeply, experience yourself as the perfect channel between these powerful energies. With each inhale, draw energy in from heaven and earth meeting in

your heart center. With each exhale, expand the energy outwards.

5. Place your hands over your heart and choose to repeat one or more of the following:

   I feel the primal pulse of the earth grounding me.

   I feel the connection to heaven expanding my spirit.

   I am rooted.

   I am safe.

   I am supported.

   I am connected to all that is.

   I am loved.

   I stand tall, as a true Empress, fully present, powerfully connected, and perfectly balanced between heaven and earth.

6. Hold this position for several breaths, anchoring this feeling of balanced power in your body's memory.

Practice this alignment daily, and notice how standing as the bridge between Heaven and Earth transforms not only your posture but your presence in the world.

CHAPTER 7

SACRED BALANCE: CREATING SPACE FOR WHAT TRULY MATTERS

The true abundance of an Empress isn't measured by what she possesses, but by the balance she creates between having enough and creating space to explore new possibilities and discover what enriches her soul. At any stage in life, it's a good idea to rethink our relationship with "things" — all those items that we have accumulated over the years and continue to purchase before decluttering or releasing what no longer serve us. An Empress knows this wisdom. She isn't attached to every possession she owns. Instead, she regularly donates and releases material items to create healthy flow in her physical and energetic space. She values space — space to breathe, space to move freely, and space to welcome new possibilities.

Like many women, I find shopping enjoyable, particularly at local discount fashion or home decorating stores. I love to purchase new items or fun accessories to wear or decorative home items. However, I've learned that the real work isn't in the acquiring – it's in what comes next. The challenge lies not in purchasing but in letting go of items. This is where a mindset shift is necessary. I have a genuine question for you: Do you want to spend more time decluttering and straightening up your environment or more time doing things that you love? Do you value time with objects or time to create new experiences?

My own journey with possessions has deep roots in my childhood, where scarcity shaped my relationship with things. My father was a barber, and we lived from paycheck to paycheck in a modest household where every purchase required careful consideration. My mother, having grown up with even less, had developed appreciation for "special" possessions that were very precious to her. She kept her fine dishes (not even china) and linens hidden away in closets, saving them for special occasions. When she passed away at only forty-nine, those cherished items remained barely used. This became a powerful lesson for me; life is too short, and we need to live unattached to our possessions.

I have spoken to many women who hold on to things because of the memories that they invoke — baby clothes, accumulated Christmas ornaments, clothes that no longer fit or are out of style. I confess that I was one of those women. During my corporate years, my closet showcased suits from Anne Klein (thanks to my friend's employee discount). I was wearing styles featured in fashion magazines. Those perfectly fitted suits made me feel incredible, and letting go of them later seemed impossible. The styles and shapes had similar silhouettes to the ones worn by Melanie Griffith in the movie Working Girl. I loved wearing power suits because they carried the energy of my identity as an ambitious, young corporate female.

It was hard to let go of them. The yellow linen blazer with the black skirt. The houndstooth pink and white suit and coordinating blouse. I can still see myself wearing them, striding confidently through those corporate hallways. Eventually, I realized I no longer needed to be attached to clothing to feel ambitious and successful. I donated them to women who needed them but couldn't afford them.

Today, my approach to clothing is different. I keep items that make me feel good — pieces that fit my physique and are also comfortable. I don't follow a specific style. I have a wardrobe that's versatile and somewhat eclectic. On most days I'm seen in jeans and a fun top but always neat and put together. I can feel like an Empress no matter what I'm wearing. Being an Empress is about choosing pieces that truly serve me rather than holding onto items for what they once represented.

As an Empress, I prefer simplicity. This philosophy extends to my skin care and makeup routine, which I've learned to simplify. My skin care is a priority, so I would prefer to invest in products that are appropriate for my specific needs rather than accumulating a variety of products. What I've discovered is that if you find something that works, stick with it. Since Covid, my makeup routine has become even more minimal — sometimes a dash of lipstick and mascara is all I need. I've embraced the approach that less is more.

These mindful choices have become part of what I call "regal rituals" — simple techniques that can become part of a regular routine, intentional practices that honor your sacred space and yourself. Regal rituals are small, meaningful acts of self-care that remind you of your inherent worth. They might include lighting a candle while you work, placing fresh flowers on your desk weekly, enjoying a cup of herbal tea before bed, or taking three deep breaths before entering your home each day. These aren't grand gestures but consistent choices that say, 'I am worthy of beauty, attention, and care.'

One of my favorite regal rituals involves my wardrobe: if I buy something new, I donate something I no longer need. Sometimes, I donate more than I purchase, and my closet reflects this balance — lush with items I love and space for the clothes to breathe instead of being jammed together. Respect the clothes and they'll respect you back with fewer wrinkles!

This practice has also made me more mindful about my purchasing decisions. I often ask myself if I really need something or if I'm purchasing something to fill an emotional void. When you spend money on things without genuine need, you must ask yourself why. What is your motivation to shop or buy? Why buy a third soy candle for the bedroom when you haven't lit any of the others? Why purchase a fifth pair of cowboy boots? (I admit, I do love cowboy boots). Ask yourself whether you are bored or trying to fill an emptiness or absence. Sometimes we shop when we're feeling unseen, unheard, or undervalued – seeking external validation through acquisition when what we really need is to honor our own worth. Purchases can provide a momentary thrill but often end up gathering dust or forgotten in the back of the closet.

I often visit stores to browse with no intention of purchasing; it's just a little escape. Frequently, I'll place items in my cart only to return them to the shelves before leaving after reconsidering the purchase. If I do purchase something I make it a habit to clear out something that I no longer need. I don't like having too many objects cluttering my environment because I know, all too well, that clutter makes me feel overwhelmed and anxious. I can sense the stagnant energy in my home and feel it in my body.

This physical reaction is explained by Traditional Chinese Medicine, which teaches that stagnant energy can lead to physical and emotional imbalances. Clutter disrupts energy flow, forcing it to get stuck in and around the objects and corner. When we remove things, the energy flows better — not just within the house but within ourselves. We need to keep our physical and energetic spaces clear of stagnant energy so that we can live more harmoniously.

One ancient practice that addresses this energy flow is feng shui, the art of intentional placement. This practice works specifically with energy flow principles. Having too many objects can create unhealthy energy patterns, blocking the natural circulation that provides vitality in our environments. When we intentionally remove things and rearrange spaces according to feng shui principles, we revitalize our environment.

Certain areas of our homes correspond to different aspects of our lives, such as — wealth, fame, relationships, children, helpful people, career, helpful people, children, and health — making mindful arrangement even more important. An Empress understands that decluttering becomes not just a household chore but a regular ritual that can shift the vibration throughout her living space and her life. This aligns perfectly with the Empress philosophy that by creating space for energy to flow freely, we invite in new possibilities to enter our kingdom.

I have practiced the art of feng shui for many years, regularly rearranging items in my home as well as updating color schemes. I find it fascinating that we can assist the flow of energy by merely moving a piece of furniture to another location. It is a great tool to help transform the energy of your home or spaces.

In my late thirties, I owned a home in the suburbs of New Jersey. It was built in the 1930s and I filled it with a few antiques and experimented with different decor. During this time, I was single, focusing on my career as a consultant and enjoying life at home with my dog, Buddy. I dated occasionally and regularly got together with friends, but what I truly wanted was a partner. At thirty-six years old I wasn't getting younger, and I wanted to start a family. While I hadn't had much luck with past relationships, I had gained wisdom and was ready for a new chapter in my life. Despite creating a beautiful home and fulfilling career, something still felt missing — that sense of connection that I deeply longed for. I began to wonder if there was something I could do to manifest this.

I hired a feng shui specialist to come into my home and give me advice. She did a special chart based on my birthdate and the direction that my house was facing. She recommended several changes that would create the energy to bring in a proper relationship. I incorporated the feng shui remedies that she recommended. Several months later, I started consulting for a company where I met my husband, Brian. We were friends at first, gradually building connection while working side by side on a project. A few months before my contract ended, our professional relationship blossomed into something more, and we started dating. The rest, as they say, is history.

Clutter extends beyond physical items. Women often take on too many roles — mother, sister, girlfriend, and cheerleader — accumulating tasks until there isn't any space in our schedules for ourselves. Learning to say no becomes easier when we embody Empress energy. It's about being discerning with what we choose into our lives. We don't need to do it all because we are afraid of judgement or losing our identity as a reliable people pleaser. When we take on too much without self-care, our bodies send clear warnings: exhaustion, headaches, backaches, and other symptoms signaling we need to pause and restore. An Empress recognizes these signals and honors her limits, claiming her throne and the sacred time she deserves.

Sometimes, we don't realize that we're overextending ourselves until we're burned out. Burnout isn't just feeling tired — it's that deep exhaustion that penetrates every fiber of your being, leaving you feeling emotionally depleted and spiritually empty. You might find yourself irritable over minor things or struggling to concentrate. Some women thrive under pressure while others require structured days with more pauses to replenish their energy. Your body will let you know when it needs to rest or when you are doing too much. Honoring its messages and give yourself the self-care that you deserve.

This personal awareness extends to our physical surroundings as well. While numerous books discuss minimizing and decluttering and living a more simplistic lifestyle, suggesting our lives become richer with less, it's important to recognize that "too much" is subjective. What I consider manageable might feel overwhelming to someone else. Finding your own comfortable balance is what matters most.

When I worked as a real estate agent, I witnessed firsthand how possessions affect space and energy. I walked into homes so filled with belongings that I found it difficult to breathe. As the seller's agent, I encouraged homeowners to declutter to get their homes market-ready, but many didn't have the energy or resources to painstakingly sort through and release their accumulated possessions. The contrast was striking: well-staged homes with minimal furniture and decorative items felt open and inviting, while cluttered spaces left potential buyers unable to envision themselves living there. I watched sellers struggle to let go of things, which often prevented their houses from selling in a timely manner. This experience taught me the importance of releasing possessions as we prepare for a time in our lives when we need less.

This process of releasing what no longer serves us, while beneficial, isn't always easy. Decluttering can be overwhelming and even frightening, especially if we haven't done it in a while. It requires both mental and physical energy, and we may not know where to begin. We can start small — a drawer, a closet, a single room. We don't have to tackle everything at once, and we shouldn't expect ourselves to start big. We may feel ready to begin decluttering immediately, or we may need time to work up to it.

We can create a gentle system of releasing and giving away, remembering that we can't hold on to anything forever. The key is being honest with ourselves without falling into guilt. If something brings us joy or serves a purpose, we should keep it. If it's something we don't even notice anymore — something that has become invisible in our daily lives — then it's time to let it go.

Think of the food you buy and consume. Once it has nourished your body it has fulfilled its purpose. The same principle applies to many possessions in your life. Initially, these items serve you, bring pleasure, and fulfill a specific need. Yet, over time, you barely notice they're around or they've outlived their purpose. While sentimental items deserve keeping, keep in mind the wisdom of letting go and that there's no storage unit in the afterlife.

Remember, dear Empress, you don't have to do everything at once. Like any practice of sovereignty, this is a journey of gradual mastery. Trust your intuition about what to keep and what to release. Your space should feel like a sanctuary that supports your highest expression of Empress energy — filled with items you truly love and use, with plenty of room for energy to flow freely. As you thoughtfully arrange your environment, you create conditions for peace, creativity, and renewed purpose to thrive in your daily life.

YOUR ROYAL INVITATION

SACRED SPACE CLEARING

As an Empress claiming your sovereign space, you understand that true abundance flows not from your belongings but honoring what truly matters in life.

The following ritual transforms decluttering from a mundane task into a meaningful practice that acknowledges both the practical and emotional aspects of letting go.

Start with a sense of purpose rather than pressure. Take one small, meaningful step at a time, knowing that each creates more clarity in your space and life. Begin in one room or area of your home. Place before you three containers: a beautiful basket for items to keep, a box for donations, and a container for items that need to be discarded. As you sort through your possessions, consider the following:

- If you needed to pack up your home tomorrow and could only take 25 percent of your belongings, what would you keep? What does this reveal about what truly matters?

- Which garments in your wardrobe no longer reflect who you are today? What identity are you holding onto through these items?

- What possessions (gifts, family heirlooms, expensive purchases, etc.) are you keeping out of obligation or guilt?

- What are you saving for "someday" that has remained unused for years?

- Which items connect you to past versions of yourself that you have gracefully outgrown

At the end of your sacred space clearing, release the energy of the items that you're discarding or donating by saying the following: "Your purpose is complete. I release you with gratitude."

Full Moon Release

The full moon has long been recognized as a powerful time for release and letting go. Just as the moon reaches its fullest expression before beginning to wane, this lunar phase offers us the perfect opportunity to identify what we've outgrown and consciously choose to release it.

Use a section of your Empress journal specifically for this purpose. This ritual works best when performed during the 2 days surrounding the full moon, when lunar energy is at its peak. You might choose to do this practice monthly, creating a beautiful rhythm of conscious release that supports your ongoing transformation.

Setting Your Sacred Space: Go to your throne or sacred space where you can be undisturbed. Gather a few simple elements to enhance this ritual:

- A candle (white or any color that feels right to you)
- Your dedicated Empress journal and a pen
- Crystals or other objects that you would like to place on your alter.
- Begin by clearing the energy in your chosen space. You can open a window or just set the intention that you're clearing the space.
- Create an altar with your objects, placing them in any way that seems appropriate. You can invite in other objects that resonate with you.
- Light your candle as a symbol of illumination—bringing light to what you're ready to release. Take three deep breaths to center yourself in this sacred moment.
- Write what you're ready to release — both physical possessions and energetic burdens. Allow the candlelight to guide your reflection as you consider:

  What responsibilities are you carrying that no longer align with your highest expression?

Which relationships in your life feel energetically heavy? What would happen if you allowed them to naturally transition?

What old stories or outdated identities about yourself are you ready to release into the moonlight?

Where in your life are you saying yes when your authentic self wants to say no? How would your life feel lighter if you released the need to please everyone in your kingdom?

What past disappointments, anger, fear, or worry are you holding onto that you now choose to release?

- As you write, affirm: As the Empress of my domain, I am prepared to let go of what no longer aligns with my highest purpose. I am making space for what truly matters.

- When you've finished writing, close your journal and sit quietly for a moment, feeling the weight of what you're choosing to release. Extinguish your candle with gratitude for this sacred time of clearing and renewal.

- Extinguish the candle.

CHAPTER 8

STRAIGHTENING CROWNS: THE POWER OF WOMEN SUPPORTING WOMEN

One of my favorite memes is of two women, both wearing crowns, but one woman's crown is a bit askew. The other woman is shown straightening her crown. To me, this represents a powerful visual of how women should be supporting other women on their journey. Whether we are maidens, mothers, or Empresses, coming together as a collective can create a force that elevates the energy of the world with kindness, love, wisdom, and compassion.

Throughout history, women's journey through society has been met with restrictions, challenges, and transformations. The corporate world of the twentieth century particularly highlighted this struggle. To succeed in male-dominated workplaces, women felt they needed to adopt masculine characteristics — wearing power suits, displaying assertive behavior, and suppressing their authentic, sensitive nature to be taken seriously. Business became challenging and competitive as women fought to be seen, heard, respected and given equal opportunities. By dimming their natural feminine wisdom, intuitive abilities, and empathy in favor of traditionally masculine traits, women found themselves competing not only against men but against each other, rather than forming the solidarity that could have strengthened their collective power.

I found that to be true in my own corporate journey. In my early twenties I worked as a data entry clerk for a large New Jersey company. I was young, naïve, and ambitious. After a year I was promoted into a clerical assistant's job in the Human Resources (HR) department where I remained for several years. During that time, I went back to college and earned my bachelor's degree in business management. This degree proved valuable when applying for jobs with more earning potential. Eventually, I was promoted to corporate trainer, where I assisted in developing programs to train individuals using computers.

In the mid-1980s, with the increasing use of computers in the corporate environment, the demand for trainers grew. When I first stepped into the role as a trainer, I carried the innocent belief that women working in similar roles would be welcoming and supportive, possibly mentoring me. I envisioned a collaborative environment, sharing ideas and working well together. Reality, however, turned out to be different. Instead of finding mentorship, I encountered resistance. They hesitated to share the resources and knowledge that would help me understand their methods. As an empath and sensitive soul, this exclusion stung deeply. I had recently lost my mom to cancer, so I was already feeling lost and abandoned. I had hoped to find a connection with other women. My intuition told me that they wanted to see me fail. But I was determined to do well. I had to put my sensitivities aside and rely on my independence, resourcefulness, and motivation to succeed.

Teaching came naturally to me. I found joy in educating others on mastering computer skills and received positive feedback from students. My confidence grew along with my skills as a trainer. Over time, the imposter syndrome faded as I focused on supporting others rather than proving myself. I genuinely fell in love with educating others.

Then came corporate restructuring, a moment I remember as clearly now as the day it happened over thirty years ago. The tension in the air was palpable as an HR manager called us in one by one. When my turn came, his dismissive energy was apparent. He barely made eye contact as I sat down, and I took this as a sign that the news was unfavorable. However, I reassured myself that, regardless of the outcome, I would be okay.

Without looking at me, with eyes fixed on his papers, he said, "I am presenting you with a document offering you the position of manager of the Human Resources Information Systems department." There was a long pause, and my heart raced as he spoke, "You have twenty-four hours to think about it and give us your answer." Then he went on to say with unmistakable disdain, "The director who is offering you this position, for some reason, thinks you are qualified. I don't know why." My head was spinning as I took the paper and walked out of the room. I had thought I was going to lose my job, instead, I was being offered a significant promotion. Looking down at the offer letter, I noticed the job title and higher pay grade which would come with a substantial salary increase. A mixture of excitement and nervous energy washed over me as I contemplated both the opportunity and the challenges ahead; this role would push me to grow in ways I hadn't anticipated. I signed the agreement without needing twenty-four hours to think about it.

Once again, I went into the new job hoping for support but found myself largely alone. My predecessor, who had been promoted, offered minimal guidance, while my assistant resented me. She told me outright that she didn't want to work with me; she wanted the job herself and felt rejected when she wasn't considered for it. I felt bad but there wasn't anything I could say to soothe her feelings. I focused instead on learning my new responsibilities while gradually trying to win her over. It wasn't easy, and I eventually gained her trust by supporting her ambition to get promoted by mentoring and advocating for her. I made it a point to give her special projects and highlight her contributions to others. My efforts eventually paid off when she received the promotion she had always wanted. I genuinely wanted to support her because I understood what it felt like to not be seen or valued by other women in the workplace.

I wanted to be a leader who supports others, especially women, because I understand that sometimes we may not feel seen or heard.

The journey from feeling unsupported to becoming a source of support for others has fueled my passion for helping women discover their worth and embrace their power. I want women to own their energy, feel empowered and find practical tools like meditation, boundary-setting, regal rituals and trusting their intuition to nav-igate personal struggles. Life's challenges carry wisdom, and it is within my own journey that I came to understand the transforma-tive power of women supporting women.

Sometimes, women feel isolated when moving through life's transitions: empty nest, perimenopause and menopause, relocat-ing, and even when facing the uncertainty of reinventing them-selves. When they need someone to actively listen without offering unsolicited advice or judgement, we can be that compassionate friend. We can offer a sacred space where they can share what is weighing heavy on their minds and in their hearts. It can be heal-ing for women to be seen and heard, especially by other women be-cause we understand the unique challenges that these transitions present.

We can also offer a warm embrace when we sense they need it. For those at a distance, visualize someone you know who is going through a difficult time and send them loving and kind thoughts. Celebrate their accomplishments and milestones by genuinely ex-pressing excitement and happiness for their successes. Through these acts of authentic connection and validation, we help women recognize their worth and ascend to their rightful thrones.

Take a moment to reflect on a time in your life when you stood alone, when support felt distant or nonexistent. How did you feel? What emotions stirred up in you? Where did you seek guidance and support? Sometimes, even as an Empress, you must know when to reach out to others and seek assistance. Recognizing when your cup needs filling is equally important. For some women, including your-self perhaps, that may be difficult. You've spent years supporting others, raising your children, helping your partners and loved ones, but it's just as important for you to ask for help. Cultivating your own circle of Empresses — women you can reach out to whenever you need guidance or just to share some good news — becomes not just important but essential to your social well-being.

I believe that today we are witnessing an evolution of more women supporting women. More women are coaching others through various life stages and mentoring younger women in their careers. We are the bridges of wisdom that connect generations. This is the true essence of being an Empress — using our wisdom and illuminating the path for others. The lessons from our own stories and struggles can become someone else's lifeline. Being an Empress is about creating sisterhood. This is how we can change the story — not by competing but by collaborating. There's no need to climb alone when we can lift each other as we rise.

As an Empress, you have the power to create a welcoming space in your kingdom that embraces and uplifts other women. Through your words, intentions, and radiant energy, let them know there is room for them to walk beside you. When we straighten each other's crowns — helping others rise as we have risen — we create a powerful network of Empresses.

YOUR ROYAL INVITATION

Reflect on your journey of giving and receiving support as an Empress. Use these questions as guides for reflection but trust your intuition about which areas need your attention most.

REFLECTION ON SUPPORT

Recall a time in your life when you felt unsupported. What type of support would you have welcomed?

- Identify three areas in your life where you need support right now.
- Who in your life supports you?
- How do you support others?
- Who in your circle is struggling right now? Can you offer them support or assistance?

BUILDING YOUR CIRCLE

- What kind of women's circle could you benefit from joining?
- Do you belong to a circle or community of women that get together regularly for tea, pickleball, book club, or another shared activity?
- Are you interested in creating a women's circle or community? How could you structure a gathering for women that creates connection?

TAKING ACTION

- Identify three women you could reach out to this week for coffee, tea, or just conversation.

- Choose one woman in your life whose crown may need straightening. Reach out to her this week with a message of support, a listening ear, or practical assistance. Notice how this act of supporting another Empress also strengthens your own sovereignty.

Through these acts of mutual support, you embody the true essence of Empress energy – lifting others as you rise, creating a legacy of sister-hood that transforms the world one crown at a time.

CHAPTER 9

THE EMPRESS'S TIME: CHOOSING WHAT DESERVES YOUR ENERGY

An Empress is intentional with her time because she knows it is her most precious resource. She deliberately chooses how and where to direct her energy, planning her days with purpose rather than simply reacting to demands. The quality of our attention determines our experience of time itself.

When we slow down and savor each moment, time seems to expand around us. But when we rush frantically from one task to the next, we find ourselves trapped in a race against time. We constantly tell ourselves that there's so much to do and so little time. Though we know that we only have so many hours in a day and limited energy to spend, we often continue cramming in more activities, more commitments, and more distractions. The truth is this. What we do with our time is our choice. Becoming aware of these choices is the first step in valuing and claiming our time.

Putting this awareness into practice, I have learned to slow down and look at what I'm inviting into my life. I often ask whether an existing task or a new one is worthy of my time. Obviously, there are obligations like work, doctor's appointments, and family commitments, but noticing where I spend my time and how I feel about what I'm doing reveals what's truly important. An Empress values her time as the precious resource it is, managing her schedule rather than letting it manage her.

Personally, as I age, I find myself embracing new experiences. I'm not slowing down, instead, I've discovered a renewed purpose while working on numerous projects that I'm passionate about. I have many dreams and goals, and I bet you do too. You may even have a vision board of what you want to accomplish and where you want your journey to take you. But to be able to do what you truly want, you may have to let go of things that are depleting your energy and not serving your highest good. You know that time is finite, so you must be decisive about what truly deserves your attention.

When we were younger, we had all the time in the world — or we thought we did. Then, as we took on more responsibilities in our work and family life, our focus changed. Our calendars filled up, leaving less time to do things that we enjoyed. For me, raising a family was enjoyable but hard work. With kids, I spent most of my time taking care of my family's needs and less on myself. I became a mom at the age of forty-one and the first two years of my twins' lives were a blur. It was a whirlwind of sleepless nights, constant feedings, and diaper changes. I went from one thing to another without pause. The next thing I knew they were all grown up and off to college. It's as if time sped up when I wasn't looking.

I'm sure you've experienced it. One moment you are graduating from high school and the next moment you're going through menopause. Time has a way of slipping through our fingers faster than we ever imagined it would. We can't bring back time, but we can be grateful for our memories and experiences and bring our attention to the present moment. We can also learn to make intentional choices on how we spend our precious time now.

When I immerse myself fully in the present moment, something magical happens. Time seems to slow down, and I enter a state of natural flow. Instead of rushing to the next task or allowing my mind to race ahead, I settle into the present moment — a rhythm of now. When I maintain this presence, I can work with greater clarity and intention. This doesn't mean my mind never wanders — when it does, I gently guide it back to focus.

This practice of presence has changed how I approach my schedule. I have become more intentional with my time, carving out space for what is important while prioritizing what needs to be done and allowing room for flexibility. Whether I'm writing, teaching, or simply enjoying a quiet moment on my throne, I'm fully engaged. This mindfulness naturally led me to become more selective about where I spend my time and energy. I'm much more mindful about taking on new projects that don't align with my purpose or when my schedule is already filled with other commitments.

This intentional approach extends beyond tasks and projects to the people in my life as well. I prioritize time with people who uplift me while limiting time with those who consistently drain my energy. This is the essence of sovereignty — claiming authority over my own kingdom. I can choose what I want to do with my time and who I want to spend it with. If you feel you don't have these same choices, I hope you'll pause and recognize your power as an Empress to shape your own schedule and relationships.

I realized how precious time is after my mother passed away at the age of forty-nine. She didn't get to experience her Empress years. She didn't get to hold her grandchildren or grow old with my father. Knowing all she missed made me determined to live differently — to value each moment and make conscious choices about how I spent my precious time.

This awareness became even more obvious when I was diagnosed with breast cancer, just one month shy of my forty-ninth birthday — the same age my mother was when she died. This coincidence became my wake-up call to slow down, carefully evaluate where I was spending my time and energy and focus more intentionally on my personal well-being. With seven-year-old twin boys depending on me, I wanted to be around for a long time to guide and witness the men they would become. I knew I had to become much more intentional about where I directed my precious energy.

The most valuable lesson I've learned through these experiences is to trust my intuition when deciding where to invest my energy. You have the same power. When faced with a new opportunity or request, go to a quiet place within yourself — your inner throne — and simply ask if this deserves your time and energy. Listen to how your body responds. Take your time before saying yes when you may need to say no. Your inner wisdom knows which commitments will drain you and which will fulfill you. This is how an Empress chooses what truly deserves her time.

Digital Connections

Consciously choosing to slow down can regulate our nervous system. When we exist in a heightened state of activity, our nervous system mirrors that intensity, often triggering anxiety, overwhelm, and even physical depletion over time. The challenge we face is a society that expects constant connectivity — immediate responses and endless scrolling. We must break the cycle by consciously slowing down and acknowledge that it's okay not to always have a device in our hands. Let's give ourselves permission to put it down and walk away.

I am guilty of digital distraction too. That familiar alert on my phone triggers an immediate response: I reach for it to see what's waiting. What begins as checking one notification often leads to scrolling through social media or catching up on emails, consuming far more time than intended. Perhaps someone posted a photo of their dog (I love those) or a funny video and suddenly I've fallen down the rabbit hole of digital distractions. Before I realize it, I've spent several hours a day on my devices. Honestly, during this time in my life, do I have the luxury of spending precious moments mindlessly scrolling my phone and responding to its every beck and call? (Pun intended!)

Digitally detoxing is a great exercise that you can do regularly to cut down the amount of time you're spending on any device from the phone to your favorite binge-worthy TV shows. The occasional tech-free hour or two can have many benefits. You can experience less tension in the body — especially in our shoulders and neck — less eye strain, better sleep, and improved mental clarity. You may also find yourself more present and engaged with the people and activities right in front of you.

One regal ritual that I started doing when I need to focus on my work is to put my phone in another room. This way it doesn't distract me with its constant alerts. So many people are attached to their phone, walking around with it in their hands as if it's an extension of their bodies. They take it from place to place. Have you ever frantically looked for your phone, only to discover that it's already in your hand? It's almost comical, yet it reveals how dependent we've become on these devices? Keep in mind how precious our time is and then consider whether spending it on your phone or other devices for several hours a day is worth it.

Speaking of better sleep, taking devices to bed can stimulate the nervous system, making it difficult to settle into a restful state. Create an atmosphere conducive to relaxation by being mindful about screen use. You can still enjoy your device, but consider limiting time and choosing gentler content; personally, I find intense dramas disruptive rather than relaxing. If screen time genuinely helps you wind down, continue that ritual, but consider adding other practices that signal to your body it's time to rest —gentle yoga or qigong, stretching, journaling, soothing music or a cup of herbal tea.

Digitally detoxing can be met with withdrawal symptoms. Fidgeting, not knowing what to do with our hands, and feeling anxious are normal. Attempting to change habits that have been a part of our lives for a long time can come with challenges like when someone quits smoking or drinking alcohol. Many former smokers report how their bodies signaled to them when it was time for a cigarette — after meals, during stressful moments, or at specific times of the day. These triggers became powerful cues. The longer they went without one, the more anxiety they felt, though these sensations gradually faded with time. Quitting isn't easy, but it's a choice made for a healthier life. Similarly, creating distance from our devices may be uncomfortable at first, but it's a choice we can make for a more present life.

Time is a precious resource and how you choose to spend it can reflect some of your values. Whether it's nurturing family, connecting with friends, or carving out time for personal growth, these choices don't just fill your calendar, they shape the story of your life. While you cannot change yesterday's chapters, you can still write tomorrow's pages. Think about your legacy. Do you want to be remembered as someone who was always on their phone or computer and didn't spend time with family and friends? Or do you want to be remembered for the radiant energy and wisdom that you embodied as an Empress?

The key lies in embracing each moment fully. When you're with family and friends, be present. Transform routine tasks like cooking dinner into opportunities for more engagement by noticing and enjoying the experience of preparing a meal. Cooking might not be your thing, but perhaps you have a different activity that calls to you. I'm inviting you to enjoy being in the moment while doing whatever you love — whether that's gardening, walking, or simply sitting with a cup of coffee. And especially when you are having conversations, be sure to actively listen and lean into the beauty of genuine connection. If you notice yourself becoming distracted, use it as a gentle reminder to pause, refocus, and return to mindful awareness.

Let's slow down, dear Empress, and be present. Find joy in the small things. Notice what and who is around you. Explore the beauty in all living things. Take long, slow breaths and feel their energy in your body. You may find that time stands still for just a moment.

YOUR ROYAL INVITATION

SCHEDULE ASSESSMENT

Take time to review your schedule. Understanding how we spend our moments is the first step toward living intentionally. Whether you prefer a paper planner or a digital one, regular review is essential. I personally use both. I like paper planners for the way it provides a visual layout of my schedule, making it easier for me to look for gaps or opportunities. I may color code my appointments to make them more distinguishable. I also use a digital planner on my phone which makes my calendar more accessible. The key isn't what type of planner you have, but in the art of reflection.

Look back at how you've spent your days recently. Did you carve out time to sit on your throne for self-reflection? Did you make space to do things that are fun alongside your work commitments? It's important to create balance in your days. Notice patterns or areas where you can make adjustments to your daily or weekly routines. If you have a busy schedule, make sure you intentionally block out time for self-care — and remember, you don't need to explain or justify this to anyone. You are in charge of your own time. This balance of work and play serve a greater purpose — experiencing harmonious and healthy energy in your life.

Allocate time to go outside for a walk or a movement practice. Even gentle stretching for twenty minutes in the morning or evening is better than no movement. As we age, it's important to move the body to help lubricate the joints and stretch the connective tissue —without this we can feel increasingly stiff and restricted in our daily activities. Doing some exercises that engage the muscles is also important to prevent atrophy. We want to incorporate healthy lifestyle choices that help us stay strong, flexible and mobile.

Additionally, carve out time for an unplugged walk. Tuck your phone in your pocket but don't use it to call anyone or browse while you're walking. Stand upright with your head lifted — this not only prevents the forward curvature of your neck and spine that comes from constantly looking down, but also opens your perspective to the world around you. Take a stroll around your neighborhood and notice what you see in terms of objects, colors, and textures. You may notice something new or meet new people in your neighborhood. Open your senses to the world around you.

THE TEN-MINUTE PERCH MEDITATION

This meditation will help you stay centered by creating a "perch" of awareness that you return to whenever your mind wanders — just like a bird in flight that eventually needs to land on its perch to rest and observe.

Instructions:

1. Start small: Begin with five minutes of focused attention and gradually increase the time as you become more comfortable with the practice.

2. Find your space: Choose a quiet place where you can be undisturbed.

3. Center yourself: Take a few deep, centering breaths, inhaling and exhaling slowly.

4. Begin the practice: Close your eyes and begin noticing or "noting" whatever arises in your awareness.

5. Practice noting: When sensations arise — like an itch on your skin or a sound — simply note them mentally by saying to yourself "itch" or "sound." If you become distracted, you can return to your breath by noting "breath."

6. Return to your perch: Remember that you are using this "noting" as your perch — your place of rest and

observation, just like a bird returning to its favorite branch.

The more you practice this simple meditation, the more you will notice that the spaces between thoughts will increase. It is within these quiet gaps — when the mind's chatter settles — where some of the most profound ideas can surface.

CHAPTER 10

AWAKENING TO POSSIBILITY: DISCOVERING POTENTIAL IN YOUR NEXT CHAPTER

Change is constant. As women who have navigated multiple decades, multiple roles, and countless transitions, this truth resonates deeply within our souls. Ancient teachings remind us that impermanence is woven into the fabric of our lives. Every ending creates new possibilities, and every challenge opens a door to unexplored opportunities. Although change can feel disruptive and not always welcomed, it can also be exciting. When you shift your perspective about change — seeing it as a partner in life's flow — you see the power in its transformation. Instead of resistance, you create collaboration. Instead of fear, you cultivate curiosity.

This is the way of the Empress. When you step fully into your sovereignty, your courage, radiance, and willingness to embrace change becomes a beacon of light for others. Your transformation encourages other women to follow in your footsteps, creating positive change that extends far beyond yourself. Like ripples in a pond, one woman's awakening inspires countless others to begin their own journey of transformation.

You can view change as a gateway that transitions you from one place to another, or from one way of being to another. You undergo change constantly, but some experiences have a larger impact on your life. Change can bring up various emotions from fear, worry, joy, and many more. Your reactions and how you manage change can directly affect the quality of your life. When you constantly resist or fear change, you prevent yourself from experiencing something potentially life altering.

Life is a continuous journey of change. Think about it: You aren't the same person that you once were. Your likes and dislikes have evolved. Your priorities, relationships, and where you now live may have changed. Tomorrow you may change your mind about something you had it set on. As an Empress, you have a right to change your mind without explanation, without apology, and without seeking anyone's permission. This doesn't mean breaking commitments to others – it means claiming your sovereignty over your own evolution and choices.

Change can be a choice, a twist of fate or a natural progression. Many women experience the joy and the challenges that motherhood brings. We go from taking care of ourselves to the responsibility of taking care of another human being. That transformation arrived in my life with the premature birth of my twin boys who weighed a little over two pounds each. Before their arrival, I had never even changed a diaper! Now I had double the work and felt blessed beyond measure. Those earlier days were a blur of learning, adapting and discovering reserves of strength and stamina I never knew I possessed. While there were certainly challenging moments of exhaustion and uncertainty, I found myself treasuring the small, ordinary miracles — their first smiles, every ounce they gained, their smell, and just the joy of being a mom to my boys.

Looking back now, I realize how swiftly those twenty plus years have passed. If you have children, I'm guessing you might have had a similar experience. You spend years pouring energy into raising your children, yet there comes a time when they must venture out on their own. That's a big change, not only for them but for us, and you knew that it would one day come. I have met many women who have tried to keep their flock home for as long as they can because they don't want to feel purposeless or alone. They've devoted most of their time to raising their children without ever seeking purpose outside of that. For those women, reframing the narrative can be helpful. Rather than seeing this change as an empty nest, I recommend thinking of it as an opportunity to explore and spread your own wings. Change is inevitable, and how you frame that change determines whether you see it as a loss or liberation.

Retirement presents another pivotal moment in your life journey. While some embrace this change with open arms others do not. It's all in the way it is perceived. You might choose to view yourself as retired from "raising children" only to redirect your energy toward a passion project. You may be retired from one career and now want to have fun and enjoy life. For some, retirement is uninvited through corporate downsizing or health concerns. Retirement can mean something different for everyone. Some people never want to retire because they feel that their life may be over and won't feel needed anymore. Or, perhaps, they were so absorbed in their work that it became their identity. Retirement doesn't have just one definition.

In fact, the very word *retirement* fails to capture the vibrant potential of this chapter in life. I feel retirement deserves a new word: *reinvention!* This phase of life isn't about stopping. It's about transforming. Every skill and experience that you've gained becomes the foundation of your next chapter. Whether it's serving on a school board, mentoring at the YMCA, or discovering entirely new passions, this transition opens doors to entirely new opportunities.

Like the butterfly's metamorphosis, any change requires patience and gentleness with yourself. When a caterpillar enters its chrysalis, it doesn't rush the transformation. It can't. It surrenders to a process that unfolds in its own time. Each stage is essential, from the darker stages in its cocoon to the time it emerges with wings. Butterflies are a symbol of change and transformation. We often resist change by clutching on to something that may no longer serve us. True freedom comes when we release our grip, trust the process, and wait for the ability to spread our beautiful wings.

When the universe creates a new opportunity and we take it, life is no longer the same. I worked for many years as a full-time employee implementing HR and payroll systems. Eventually I wanted to explore different opportunities and start my own consulting business. I remember feeling both excited and anxious. That feeling of butterflies in my stomach was a signal to me that change would be good. I needed to move out of my comfort zone and explore other opportunities that would take me there. Although I was nervous, wondering how quickly I would find work and how long it would last, I took the leap and I'm happy that I did. It was an incredible time in my life, and I grew both personally and professionally.

Sometimes change is forced upon us. The loss of a job, the loss of a loved one, or a medical diagnosis can change your life. Since my mom passed away from cancer, I make sure that I get regular breast exams. One year, my OB/GYN nurse practitioner told me to see a breast surgeon because I had dense breasts and a history of breast cancer in my family. My breast surgeon recommended yearly MRIs in addition to my mammogram. It may sound excessive, but it saved my life. During the first MRI two lumps were found. Both were biopsied and found to be cancerous.

I received the call a few days after Christmas. When I hung up the phone, a feeling of numbness came over me. Tears came down my face as I replayed the doctor's words in my mind: "I'm sorry. You have cancer. Make an appointment to come in and we'll discuss your options." My dog, Buddy, knew something was wrong and came over to comfort me. So many thoughts and scenarios were playing out in my head. My mom died at forty-nine, and here I was, diagnosed just one month shy of my forty-ninth birthday. I had sworn I would get past forty-nine without cancer and live a long life. Now I imagined the worst. What was I going to do?

That's when it hit me. I got up off the floor, brushed myself off (literally because dog hair was all over me), and said out loud, "I've got this. I have two young kids, and I'm going to be around for a very long time. I still have so much to do in my life and so much to live for." I was scared but it was in my nature to stay positive.

My breast cancer diagnosis and recovery became a transformative passage in my life, a threshold through which I emerged into a new way of being. It served as a profound wake-up call. While my body transformed, adapting to the changes brought by surgery, tamoxifen and early menopause, I learned to embrace this metamorphosis. Rather than resist my changed body and circumstances, I cultivated deeper self-love and compassion throughout my healing journey. This gentle acceptance, coupled with maintaining hope and gratitude, enabled me to fully return to living. Instead of viewing myself as a victim, I focused on the blessing that my cancer was discovered early. Through this experience, I discovered strength I didn't know I possessed and a deeper appreciation for life's precious moments.

Each transition, each change, each new beginning is an opportunity to grow. Embracing the transition to Empress can bring up feelings about nearing the end of our life, about no longer being worthy or valued. These feelings are valid, but they are far from the truth. Many of these feelings originate in what our culture puts on us. By embracing the transition to Empress, we are inviting new ways to explore, new ways to grow, and new ways to live a richer life. We are rewriting the rules of aging.

YOUR ROYAL INVITATION

As you step into your sovereign power to navigate change, use these prompts to examine your relationship with transformation and discover the wisdom you've already gained through life's transitions.

REFLECTION JOURNAL PROMPTS

- What patterns do you notice in how you typically react to change?

- Describe a change you resisted that ultimately led to growth.

- What upcoming change makes you most anxious right now? List your biggest fears about this change. What actions can minimize these fears? What positive outcomes can come out of this change?

- What resources or support system do you have that can help you navigate major changes?

PRACTICE CONSCIOUS CHANGE

Shake it up! You can practice embracing change by trying something new. Something amazing may happen, but if it doesn't, then you have at least taken a brave step beyond your comfort zone. Even something like a watercolor painting class, especially if you've never considered yourself artistic, can help you learn something new about yourself.

Trying new things can create conscious change in the way you do things. For example:

SMALL SHIFTS:

- Take a new route to work
- Try a different exercise routine (belly dancing, Pilates, Zumba)
- Try a new cuisine
- Reconnect with someone from your past

BIGGER LEAPS:

- Go back to school or take a college course
- Learn a new technical skill (coding, digital photography, social media)
- Start a podcast or blog
- Launch a small business or side hustle
- Join a new club or community group
- Start a creative project outside of your comfort zone
- Take on a leadership role in your community
- Learn a new language
- Plan a solo adventure or trip

After you try some things, evaluate the changes. Ask yourself how you felt, what you experienced, and start making a list of new things that you may want to explore.

CHAPTER 11

AN EMPRESS'S INNER VOICE: CONNECTING WITH YOUR SACRED INTUITIVE WISDOM

An Empress embodies wisdom that goes far beyond her intellect. She possesses an innate connection to divine guidance that whispers truth through her very being. This sacred knowing — this intuition — is one of her most powerful gifts. When she learns to trust and honor this inner compass, it becomes her most trusted advisor in all aspects of life.

In guiding decisions, her intuition cuts through the noise of what she should do and what is expected of her to what is aligned with her deepest truth. It's the quiet voice that says "wait" when she would normally rush forward. Her intuition can act as an early warning system alerting her to energies that don't serve her and helping her create boundaries that honor her sacred space and show her where to invest her precious energy.

This connection to inner wisdom isn't just a gift, it's a birthright that every woman carries within her. My own journey of discovering and trusting this divine guidance began early in life, through an experience that would forever change how I understood the power of intuitive knowing.

I first realized that I had a strong intuition when I was ten. My family often traveled from New Jersey to Brooklyn on the weekends to visit family, gathering around to share stories and an Italian meal. It was Memorial Day. I was having fun playing with my cousins, but

105

the entire time I felt an uneasy sensation in my stomach. I had a strong sense that my family would get into an accident on the way home. This knowing was certain, and it stayed with me the entire day. I didn't tell anyone. I didn't know what to say, and I didn't think anyone would believe me. I tried to dismiss it, but it lingered.

Around 9:00 pm we said our good-byes, which can take a while in a large family, and got into our big car. This was 1979, and many cars didn't have seatbelts back then. It was raining. I decided that I would close my eyes and try to fall asleep so that I wouldn't be awake when it happened, if anything happened at all.

I must have dozed off as intended. Suddenly, I heard my mother scream, "Watch out!" We hit a car stopped in the right lane of the Staten Island Expressway with its lights turned off. I opened my eyes and found myself sitting on the floor with a large lump on my forehead, everything fuzzy and surreal. My sister lay beside me, barely moving. My dad struggled to open our locked door until I managed to reach up and unlock it. My mom was in the front bleeding and in pain from hitting the windshield, which had cracked on impact.

People stopped to help amid the chaos as pain radiated from my left hip. Soon the ambulance arrived, taking us to a Staten Island hospital where I'd spend three and a half months, mostly in traction for my broken hip. My mom suffered the worst with a broken jaw, arm, and leg, requiring time in ICU. My sister broke her pelvis, and my dad had a broken nose. It was one of the worst days of our lives. As we began our journey toward healing, I couldn't stop thinking about that feeling I'd had earlier in the day — the knowing that something would happen.

The physical and emotional aftermath of that night would stay with us for years. The experience was deeply traumatic for all of us. Yet through this hardship, I discovered something important about myself: My intuition was strong. From that day forward, I made a conscious effort to listen to that inner voice. I can't always predict how my choices will affect me, but I've learned that by tuning into my intuition, I'm more likely to make decisions that align with my highest good. Even though I couldn't prevent what happened, the experience taught me to trust and stay connected to my inner guidance throughout my life.

In the years that followed, this relationship with my intuition evolved. There have been many times when I've followed my inner guidance, and others when I've ignored it. When I've dismissed those intuitive warnings, I've found myself on paths that didn't serve me well — though each detour taught me valuable lessons. Like the time I got involved in a relationship that felt wrong from the start. My intuition warned me it wouldn't be right for me, but I ignored those signals because I didn't want to be alone. I stayed far longer than I should have, enduring an increasingly abusive situation until the pain of staying finally outweighed my fear of leaving.

Fortunately, there have equally powerful times when I've honored my intuitive guidance — and those decisions have enriched my life immeasurably. Like when my inner voice nudged me to became a consultant, leading to a career that flourished. Or when my husband and I were searching for a new home, I insisted on buying this one house that required significant renovations. Despite the logical arguments against it, I was certain it would be the perfect fit for us — and it has been. These experiences taught me that this isn't about certainty — this is about trusting our inner knowing and having the courage to allow it to guide us.

We all have intuitive guidance. It can come from a feeling in your stomach or solar plexus —that chakra or energy center right below the rib cage. It could feel like a tingling on the back of your neck, a spidey sense, or a whisper in your ear from Spirit or your inner voice. Sometimes it could just be a knowing — a feeling inside that tells you whether something is right or not. These sensations manifest differently for each person and can even vary within your own experience over time. The more you listen to and trust your inner guidance, the less often you'll find yourself thinking "I should have listened to my gut."

Your body serves as one of the most powerful channels for receiving intuitive messages. Whether it's the hair raising on the back of your neck or the subtle changes in your breathing, these physical sensations are ways your intuition communicates with you. Like an antenna picking up signals (or perhaps more like a Wi-Fi connection in today's world), your energy field constantly receives information from your environment.

Over the years, I've come to understand that my intuition manifests in various forms. I found myself guided to exactly the right teachers or discovering the right books at the perfect moments. When I set the intention to deepen my understanding of spiritual concepts, new doors began opening — not just to intuitive studies, but to healing practices like Reiki. The right tools, people, and resources emerged at precisely the right moments and under ideal circumstances.

What I've learned is that our intuition is a skill that strengthens with use. Like any ability, I've been able to refine and enhance this natural gift by studying with remarkable teachers who helped me develop greater sensitivity and accuracy while learning to trust the messages received.

You can establish a connection to Spirit — your guides, angels, source, and ancestors — anyone who exists beyond the physical realm. If you believe in the afterlife, you can open yourself to receive guidance from those who have passed by asking for messages or signs of their presence. These messages may appear through symbols, dreams, feelings and visions that you experience.

One of my favorite stories about connecting with divine guidance is about my very first Reiki session. This was during my spiritual awakening when I went back home to live with my dad after a messy breakup. I was practicing regular yoga and immersing myself in different spiritual concepts from the few books that I could find, which were mostly about working with my "higher self" or Spirit guide to help me overcome self-limiting beliefs and manifest the life I wanted.

My yoga teacher at the time was also a Reiki practitioner. During class he spoke about the healing energy of Reiki and how it helped to promote a healthy flow of energy in the chakras. I became curious about this healing modality, sensing that I needed more healing energy in my life. I had been on my journey to mending my broken heart, finding inner peace, and feeling more joy. I felt physically and emotionally healthy and had a great career, but I felt that there was something missing. Although I wasn't focused on finding a long-term relationship just yet, I knew I wanted to become a mom one day and my clock was ticking.

I didn't know much about Reiki, but I intuitively felt that it was the right thing to experience, so I scheduled a session. When the day arrived, the Reiki practitioner came to the house, set up a Reiki table, and carefully explained how he would conduct the session. He told me that I might fall asleep or go into a semi-conscious state and that I might feel warm, cold, or tingly sensations. With a sense of anticipation mixed with curiosity, I then closed my eyes and the Reiki healing began. I had no idea I was about to receive a life-changing vision.

Reiki is an ancient Japanese healing technique that works with universal life force energy to promote relaxation, balance, and healing. A Reiki practitioner is attuned to the energy that flows through their crown chakra and out the palms of their hands. During my session, I slipped into a dream-like state — that peaceful space between waking and sleeping. I've always been a very visual person — often daydreaming and seeing things in my third eye. During that dream-like state, I had a prophetic vision. I saw my mom, who had already transitioned to spirit about seven years prior, come down from a higher place wearing a flowing white dress. She had a big smile and the palms of her hands were together as if in prayer. When she opened them, she revealed two baby bottles. In my soul, I knew that the vision was real and the message was clear: One day I would have twins. This wasn't just a comforting dream — it was a message from beyond.

I woke up from the session feeling very different. I felt this amazing sense of peace wash over me. I was told that in the coming days I might experience vivid dreams, colors looking more vibrant, and tears. Reiki helps to unblock energy that is stuck in the body and through this process helps release emotions. This can help heal parts of us that have experienced deep emotional pain and trauma.

I remember noticing how much brighter everything looked the next day as if my inner light was becoming more illuminated after being dim for a long time. And yes, I did cry as I released long-repressed emotions, including grief from my mom's passing. But I also felt such joy because I knew in my heart that my mom's spirit was near, and I strongly believed her message that one day I would have twins. It was such a powerful and unwavering feeling.

That feeling gave me hope. Hope that I would become a mom one day. I would tell myself that God was going to bless me with twins. Twins run in the family on my mother's side. Several years later I started dating Brian (now my husband) and I mentioned that I would someday have twins. I don't think he quite believed me until several years later when I became pregnant and, during my first scan, the doctor said we were having identical twin boys. While the doctor delivered this news as a surprise, I felt only deep confirmation. My husband just looked at me and smiled — after years of hearing me say this would happen, he wasn't shocked either.

One of the most effective ways to connect with your intuition is to cultivate a state of stillness. When you silence your internal chatter or "monkey mind," you become more receptive to perceiving, hearing, and knowing the intuitive messages that emerge. In this quiet space, without the constant noise of thoughts, worries, and mental to-do lists, your inner wisdom has room to surface. This stillness doesn't require hours of meditation — even a few minutes of deep breathing or sitting quietly can create the openness needed for intuitive insights to flow. The key is learning to trust what arises in these peaceful moments, whether it comes as a sudden knowing, a physical sensation, or a gentle inner voice. While you can use tools like oracle cards or a pendulum to enhance this practice, ultimately you know the answers. You are your own oracle, and the real skill lies in learning to trust what you receive.

What oftentimes prevents you from acting on your intuition is lack of trust in what you're feeling. Trusting your intuition can take practice. When you try to make sense out of what you're feeling and use logic to explain something, you can get in your own way. You're scrambling the intuitive messages. The key is to trust that first flash of knowing before your mind steps in to analyze. This trust builds over time, and like any relationship, the more you honor your intuition, the more it reveals itself to you.

Take a moment to reflect on your own experiences with intuition. Most of us have felt that sudden sense of knowing, experienced a déjà vu, or received what some call an intuitive "hit". Perhaps you've walked into a room and immediately sensed the mood, or met someone new and instantly felt drawn to them — or wanted to keep your distance. Maybe you've found yourself changing course at the last minute, choosing a different route home or switching your plans entirely, only to discover later that your spontaneous decision served you well. These moments aren't coincidences — they're evidence of your intuitive abilities already at work. The question isn't whether you have intuition, but whether you're paying attention to it.

These intuitive messages don't appear mysteriously; they manifest as distinct physical sensations within your body. As I mentioned previously about the chakras, your solar plexus is where you often experience a message from your intuition. This gut feeling can feel like a gentle churning, a pulling, or a sharp jolt. The intensity of these sensations often reflects how important the message is — the stronger the feeling, the more your inner guidance is urging you to pay attention.

Another chakra which serves as the center of divine vision and intuitive insight is your third eye chakra, located in the sacred space between your eyebrows. While your solar plexus speaks through physical sensations, your third eye communicates through images and visions known as clairvoyance or clear seeing. It is a kind of "seeing" that transcends your physical eyes — like watching a movie on the screen of your mind.

For some, this type of visual intuition comes naturally and feels comfortable. This gift can be cultivated and strengthened by anyone who wishes to develop it. To access this intuitive sight, find a quiet space, close your eyes, and ask yourself an important question. Then simply wait and watch. Pay attention to what appears on the screen of your inner vision. It might come as a symbol, a color, a scene, or even a complete image carrying guidance meant specifically for you. This is exactly how my mother appeared to me during that first Reiki session—a vivid, unmistakable vision that revealed a life-changing truth about my future.

While this focused practice is powerful, you don't always need a formal meditation to access your intuitive vision. Clairvoyant experiences happen during ordinary, mundane moments when your conscious mind is relaxed. When your hands are busy with routine tasks like folding laundry or washing dishes, you naturally slip into a trance-like state that opens your third eye. In this gently altered consciousness, images and visions can flow freely across your inner screen.

Daydreaming, often dismissed as distraction, is a powerful portal to this intuitive realm. During these moments when you're gazing peacefully into space or letting your mind wander, you naturally enter the perfect state for clairvoyant experiences. These visions might offer glimpses of past lessons or future possibilities. Sometimes they flash across your awareness so quickly you might miss them. By bringing gentle awareness to these seemingly idle moments, you can strengthen your connection to your inner sight. Notice the colors, textures, and scenes that naturally arise without trying to analyze their meaning. Simply allowing these visions to flow freely helps develop your clairvoyant abilities.

It's important to reduce or eliminate distractions when you are trying to receive intuitive guidance. You can deliberately and energetically connect to a higher frequency by opening your energetic pathways or chakras, specifically your crown chakra (lotus crown) which helps you connect to a higher source, whether it's God, angels, or the Universal Consciousness. Just as you would look for a clear cell phone signal for better reception, you need to clear out your internal static to hear, know, feel, and see the guidance meant for you.

If you're interested in exploring and enhancing your intuitive abilities, there are numerous books and teachers offering courses on this topic. The most important thing to remember is that you already possess the foundational intuitive gifts needed to begin this journey. When exploring your options, be discerning about which teachers and programs you choose. Tap into your inner wisdom and ask yourself if this path aligns with your true desires and aspirations. Trust your intuition and listen to the inner voice that will guide you toward the right path.

You can choose to learn more about the different *clairs* (the French word for clear) that exist. Clairs are the senses that you use to receive intuitive guidance They include the following:

- **Clairvoyance** — ability to see things in your mind's eye
- **Clairsentience** — ability to feel/sense emotional energy
- **Clairaudience** — ability to hear things

- **Claircognizance** — ability to learn information without knowing it
- **Clairalience** — ability to smell things when they're not actually physically present
- **Clairgustience** — ability to taste things without physical contact

As you go about your daily routines, use moments as opportunities to practice tuning into your intuitive guidance. When you're met with a decision, tune into your body and see how it responds to the choices you can make. Pay attention to our first instinctual reaction before your mind starts analyzing. Your intuition also activates when you encounter new people or places. Notice what you sense around you. Does something feel off? Do you feel immediately comfortable or do warning bells go off in your mind and your body?

Let's say you are offered a new job or opportunity to work on a new project. What is your initial reaction? Rather than responding immediately, go to your inner throne and tap into that guidance. Allow yourself time to sit with the question and let the answer surface. Find a quiet space to tune into your body's messages through subtle sensations. What does your gut tell you? What images or thoughts comes to mind? Do you hear a whisper in your ear telling you something?

A similar exercise can be done when meeting someone for the first time (or for the hundredth time). As you interact, you tune into the energy within their aura — the energetic space surrounding our bodies that holds information about who we are. You may sense something positive, negative, or neutral. Pay attention to what you're feeling and the quality of that sensation. Notice where you feel it in your body. That is your intuitive guidance speaking to you. By recognizing these signals regularly, you develop an intimate relationship with yourself, specifically with the part of you that always has your best interest at heart.

Like any valuable skill, your intuition can be strengthened with regular practice. An exercise that I like to use when I have a decision to make is to imagine that I'm driving up to a traffic light. First, I think about the question that I want answered. Then, I close my eyes and imagine I'm approaching a traffic light. I look up at the light and notice what color it is. If it is green, then it's a GO! If it's yellow, I take it as a sign to do more research or wait. If it is red, it means NO — I shouldn't move forward with it.

As you continue to nurture your intuition, it will become more refined and accessible. This inner wisdom — whether felt in your body, seen in your mind's eye, or heard in quiet reflection — is one of your most precious gifts as an Empress.

YOUR ROYAL INVITATION

Developing your intuition requires regular practice patience and trust in the process. Here are a few exercises or practices that you can incorporate into your sovereign practice. Use whatever resonates with you.

THE TRAFFIC LIGHT EXERCISE

This is an exercise that I learned from a teacher, and I use it whenever I need a quick answer to something. Close your eyes and imagine a traffic light with no colors lit. Ask yourself a yes/no question about a decision you need to make. The first color that appears is your answer:

- Red = Stop/No
- Yellow = Caution/Maybe
- Green = Go/Yes

DAILY STILLNESS PRACTICE

Set aside five to ten minutes each day to sit in complete silence. Focus on your breath and without judgment notice any sensations, images, or thoughts that arise. This helps clear the internal static that often blocks intuitive messages. **You can also practice the The Ten-Minute Perch Meditation from Chapter 9.**

INTUITION JOURNAL

Keep a daily journal of your gut feelings, hunches, and random thoughts. Later, go back and review which ones turned out to be accurate. This helps build trust in your intuitive abilities.

MORNING PAGES

This is a great practice that I have been doing for several years. The best time to do this is first thing in the morning — even before grabbing that first cup of coffee or tea — when you're not yet distracted or thinking too much about your day ahead.

Write down everything that comes to your mind. It doesn't have to make sense. You just need to get it on paper. It could be the dream you had the night before, what you're feeling, something silly, anything that is channeling through you. Fill up two to three pages of writing. This creates a natural flow state of thoughts and helps to create space in your mind. It is within that space that you often have your most profound thoughts.

ENERGY SENSATION

- Practice sensing the energy of spaces and people.
- Enter a room and notice your first impression.
- Meet someone new and notice your initial feeling.
- Hold an object and sense any impressions or feelings it gives you.
- Hold old photographs and notice what impressions or emotions arise.
- Practice sensing the energy of your pets or animals.

RECURRING SYMBOLS

Symbols are a big way that we can receive messages from something greater than ourselves. Psychics and mediums use symbols to provide messages. For example, birds often represent Spirit, angels, or ancestors, but they can also represent a desire for freedom or change. Pay attention to recurring signs, symbols, numbers, or patterns in daily life. Write these down in your journal. Symbols can show up as answers and signs. You can create your own symbol chart by writing down what certain ones mean to you. This can serve as a guide when you're seeking answers to questions or when they show up in visions **Common Symbolic Meanings:**

Water: emotions, cleansing, spiritual flow, or need for healing

Butterflies: transformation, rebirth, or messages from deceased loved ones

Roses: love, beauty, or spiritual protection (red = passion, white = purity, pink = gentle love)

Keys: new opportunities, solutions, or unlocking hidden potential

Bridges: transitions, connections between worlds, or crossing into new phases of life

Clocks or watches: timing issues, "time is running out," or pay attention to divine timing

Numbers: like 111, 222, 333 often signal spiritual messages or synchronicities

Feathers: angels nearby, spiritual protection, or messages from Spirit

Coins: abundance coming, value your gifts, or material concerns

Doors : new opportunities, choices to be made, or pathways opening

Hearts: love, emotional healing, or matters of the heart need attention

Stars: guidance, hope, divine connection, or your highest potential

Remember, symbols are deeply personal. A snake might represent danger to one person but transformation and healing to another. Trust your first instinct about what a symbol means to you.

CHAPTER 12

THE EMPRESS'S MIRROR: REFLECTIONS OF SELF-VALIDATION

There's an undeniable warmth that spreads through us when someone acknowledges our efforts. When we hear "Wow, that is amazing," "You did a great job," or "I really value your input," something lights up within us. It can sometimes be a turning point in the way we feel about ourselves. While this external validation feels wonderful and helps us feel valued, there's a delicate balance to maintain. When we become dependent on others' approval to feel worthy, we unknowingly give away our power. An Empress understands this distinction; she knows her inherent self-worth and recognizes that she is both valued and valuable.

Many of us grew up in environments where praise was a rare commodity. Perhaps our parents believed that praise would diminish our drive to excel, or maybe they themselves never experienced such affirmation in their own lives. Those fortunate enough to hear their parents express pride in them likely developed a stronger foundation of self-worth. In the generation of my childhood, parenting styles often emphasized that children should be quiet, neither seen nor heard unless spoken to. Yet, deep within, we all shared that universal yearning for parental pride and love — those simple words that could make us feel cared for and motivated to achieve more.

I've struggled with seeking approval throughout most of my life, especially during my early years. As a child of immigrants, I channeled my energy into being studious, independent, and self-sufficient. While I wasn't perfect, I was diligent in my work and followed the rules. I believed that achieving good grades in school would earn the validation I craved from my parents, but such grades were merely expected of me. Instead, I was largely left to do my own thing — studying, reading, writing. I often wrote short stories and poems as a way of expressing hidden emotions. The absence of phrases like "I'm proud of you" created a void within me, producing feelings of abandonment that I would later carry into relationships. I constantly battled an inner voice that whispered I wasn't good enough and didn't deserve love or kind treatment. This internal struggle manifested as excessive people-pleasing, until I lost myself in relationships and the constant drive to help and please others.

The turning point came when I recognized that many of my relationship struggles stemmed from feeling unloved, unappreciated, and undervalued. I knew that the real work was in peeling back the layers and uncovering why I craved validation so desperately. I embarked on a journey that included therapy sessions and immersing myself in books about codependency, self-love, and gratitude. I did what is considered "shadow work" —courageously visiting parts of my life that I kept hidden away, like the poems in my locked desk drawer. I discovered yoga and Reiki, which helped me shift the energy within my own body. Through these healing experiences, I discovered my path to self-awareness, self-love, and authentic fulfillment. Most importantly, I learned the transformative power of forgiveness.

The realization that change begins within us can be both empowering and overwhelming. As I reflected on my childhood, particularly my relationship with my mother, it opened old wounds. I relived moments when I felt dismissed, unsupported, lost, and emotionally abused. Of course, I remembered the times we connected, but those moments were outnumbered by times I felt isolated and alone. Since my mother had already passed when I addressed my shadow work, I was unable to have real-time conversations with her that would help me understand and address how her own mental anguish affected her parenting. Through the stories she had shared with me over the years, I understood that her upbringing in Sicily with a father who was stern and volatile had shaped her perception of raising children.

With this context about her difficult upbringing, I was able to begin my own healing journey with both clarity and compassion. As I learned to heal my wounds through therapy, I also found healing through internal dialogues with my mom in Spirit, letting her know how I felt and how I would have preferred to be treated. These heart-to-heart conversations, though one-sided, became a crucial part of my healing journey. I also found ways to communicate with my inner child, visualizing myself as a young girl who wanted to be told that she was loved. Our childhood experiences may shape our thought patterns and behaviors, but they don't have to define our future. Self-healing is an ongoing journey of discovery, teaching us how to live authentically and choose what to embrace, what to release, and how to handle the aspects of ourselves we'd rather not face.

I've been on this journey of building self-worth for many years, yet I still find myself questioning myself at times. That inner voice occasionally surfaces with judgment and criticism. While writing this book, I often questioned myself: Who am I to write this? Who will want to read this? But I reminded myself that my voice matters, that I've conquered my personal battles, and that I've claimed my throne as an Empress. Now I'm here to help other Empresses do the same, sharing the tools I've sharpened along the way.

When you consciously shift your inner dialogue from negative to positive statements, you begin rewriting your life's script. These aren't mere affirmations — they're powerful truths you've always known but perhaps never fully embraced. Rather than waiting for others to recognize your value, uniqueness, and amazing qualities, you must first acknowledge them yourself. These reclaimed truths become the foundation of your spirit, shaping how you show up for yourself and others. While transforming your inner narrative requires dedication (especially after years of self-doubt), it's essential work. Even when others praise you, the real question remains: Do you truly believe it deep within?

I developed a practice I call Value Journaling, where I list in bullet points what I value about myself and meaningful things I've done. Whether daily or weekly, I continue this practice of self-recognition rather than seeking external validation. Instead of waiting for someone else's "I'm proud of you," I acknowledge my own inherent worth. I celebrate milestones big and small. I have found this practice shifts the perspective I have about my self-worth.

When you cultivate genuine self-worth, you naturally seek less external validation in both your professional and personal life. Praise becomes a pleasant bonus rather than a necessity, and criticism loses its power to knock you off center. This is the essence of self-worth.

Another element to your sovereignty around feeling worthy is how you accept criticism and feedback. You can choose to respond with grace or with defensiveness. When someone says to me, "I enjoy your class, but I would love more of these postures," I receive it as constructive feedback, which I value and welcome. However, if someone said, "I really disliked your class. Why did you do so many downward dogs?" the criticism used to trigger my defensiveness, and I would take the remarks personally. I've learned to pause before responding to comments like these, allowing space for thoughtful reflection. I've learned that no reaction is better than a strong reaction and that taking time to formulate a response is better than shooting from the hip.

This thoughtful approach to feedback didn't come naturally. Like many women, I've been labeled "sensitive" when setting boundaries or expressing discomfort with others' behavior. For years, I internalized this label as a flaw, particularly when male figures in my life used it to dismiss my concerns. When I would say, "I don't appreciate how you spoke to me," they would respond, "Stop being so sensitive." These experiences created a cycle of feeling unworthy, undervalued, and unheard. I began to believe that sensitivity was a weakness and stopped expressing my feelings. Through healing and developing my own sense of self-worth, I transformed my approach. I learned to become more confident in setting boundaries and expressing discomfort with others' treatment of me.

This journey taught me a crucial truth — the more you hold back your words, the easier it becomes not to speak your truth. It takes practice, but as an Empress, gradually start exercising your right to be heard because, your voice matters. Your wisdom and your presence are needed. Never silence your voice, instead choose your moments wisely and always infuse your words with the energy of kindness.

While expressing your truth is essential, equally important is how you receive the words of others. As Empresses, we need not attach ourselves to others' words or expectations about our behavior. We rule our own sovereign space, which contains a rich history of beginnings and endings, successes and failures, likes and dislikes. Our experiences have given us wisdom about how to move forward and what to leave behind.

When someone offers admiration and support, respond with a gracious "thank you". When faced with unkindness, choose not to dwell on it. Don't waste your energy rehearsing imaginary conversations or scenarios. Let go of the urge to engage in power struggles. Instead, walk the path of grace, head held high, knowing your value remains constant. While this level of self-assurance doesn't come naturally at first, with practice it becomes your strength.

Each experience, whether triumph or challenge, adds to your wisdom. You move through life with dignity, knowing that your value comes from within. An Empress doesn't live to impress others, she lives to express her authentic value. With quiet confidence, she looks in the mirror and asks, "Mirror, mirror on the wall, who did a great job after all?" The answer, she knows, always reflects her own inner light.

YOUR ROYAL INVITATION

The energy of a Rising Empress means cultivating the spirit of your existence and consciously choosing how you show up for yourself and the world. I invite you to step fully into your power, release the need for external validation, and recognize that you are both valued and valuable simply because you exist.

The following practices will guide you in building a foundation of self-validation that can withstand external judgment. Choose the practices that resonate most with you, knowing that consistency is key to transformation. When your spirit needs lifting, remind yourself that you've earned your place upon the throne of your sovereign kingdom, and no one can take that away from you.

DAILY DECLARATIONS

Begin each day by declaring your worth through daily affirmations that rewrite your inner narrative. When you speak these words before your mirror, watch how your posture shifts and how your eyes begin to shine.

- I am proud of myself.
- I am valuable
- I am worthy
- I am enough
- I am unique.
- I am bold.
- I am a warrior.
- I embody wisdom.
- I am an Empress.

THE VALUE JOURNAL PRACTICE

Establish a Value Journal where you record everything you treasure about yourself. This can include:

- Daily accomplishments or achievements — both grand and humble
- Moments when courage flowed through you
- Ways you've honored your body and health
- Personal growth milestones that marked your evolution
- Qualities you admire in the Empress that you are
- Ways you've transformed pain into wisdom
- Acts of kindness you've shown to yourself and others
- Decisions you've made that honored your authentic self
- Ways you've reinvented yourself or embraced change
- Skills or talents you've developed over the years
- Challenges you've overcome and the strength they revealed
- Times you chose self-compassion over self-criticism
- Creative expressions that brought you joy

Let this journal be a testament to your journey — a treasure chest of self-validation that no one can diminish or take away.

YOUR REFLECTION SPACE

Take time to contemplate for following questions:

- What unique gifts do I bring to the world?
- How can I better honor my own wisdom?
- What declarations can I add to strengthen my self-worth?
- How will I celebrate my value today?

CHANGE YOUR INNER DIALOGUE

The most powerful transformation begins when we learn to silence our inner critic. Come up with a word or phrase that you can say to yourself to silence that voice. You might gently say, "Ssshhhh" or "Be gentle." Or you might forcefully say, "Not in my kingdom!" Be kind to yourself as you do so, recognizing that the inner voice is a buried version of your wounded child-self or someone from your past. Learn to reshape your inner voice to one that is kind and compassionate.

WHEN SUPPORT IS NEEDED

If the weight of the crown feels too heavy, if self-worth seems distant, or your inner child cries out for healing, I invite you to seek professional help or support from those you trust. Consider reaching out to another Empress in your circle — a woman who embodies the sovereignty you admire. Empresses understand that asking for support isn't weakness but an act of self-care and wisdom.

Remember, dear Empress, that self-healing is an ongoing journey. There will be moments when old doubts surface or confidence wavers. In these times, return to your Value Journal, revisit your declarations, and remember that you've earned your place upon your sovereign throne.

CHAPTER 13

THE ART OF REINVENTION: BREAKING THROUGH BARRIERS OF AGE AND EXPECTATION

Many women have been conditioned to believe that aging means stepping back, becoming invisible, or accepting a smaller version of themselves. And I'm here to tell you that entering your Empress years is your invitation to expand, explore, and embrace the most authentic and powerful version of yourself. This is the perfect time to reinvent yourself, to pursue those long-held dreams, and to harness the incredible wisdom you've gained through your journey thus far.

Stepping into a new career or trying something new can be unnerving or even scary. As a result, some of us rarely step out of our comfort zone or bubble because we're afraid that we will fail or look ridiculous. We live vicariously through others, scrolling social media and wishing we had a fun job or the courage to change our look. Perhaps we always had the desire to travel but have never been out of the state or country we're living in. Eventually we begin to feel discouraged and stuck in a pattern of not having the courage to pop the bubble.

We have been everything from daughters, wives, mothers, and friends to others. We encourage others to take a leap, but when it's our turn we're stuck in the lotus mud. Many of us lose ourselves in the roles that we've been in. We place the needs of others before us. As mothers, we spend most of our time raising our children. Even when our kids are older and don't rely on us as much, we may still want to hover over them rather than encourage their independence. We crave a sense of purpose, which often leads us to become deeply involved in our children's lives. Once they are gone from the nest, we find that it's difficult to reconnect with what we want or even know what that is. We may convince ourselves that our time for new adventures has passed. But guess what? You deserve to try something new, to reignite a passion, and to reinvent yourself.

One of the biggest fears that women have is that it's too late — too late to change careers, too late to begin working, too late to date or begin a new relationship, too late to explore her sexuality, too late to turn attention to a long-held dream. If you let fear get in the way of moving forward, you will always wonder what would have happened if you only had taken the leap. When you attempt new things and push through your fear, your confidence grows. You discover a renewed sense of excitement for life's possibilities, and those whispers of self-doubt diminish.

Society plants the seed that we are too old to embark on a new journey and that bold new moves are for the young, but that's simply untrue. The Empress years are the right time for reinvention. You have wisdom, experience, and clarity that your younger self may not have had. How many times have you said to yourself, "I wish I knew this when I was younger"? Well, dear Empress, now you do know. This is your time to use that hard-won wisdom. Every lesson learned, every challenge overcome, every moment of clarity gained — they've all been preparing you for this chapter of bold reinvention.

Exploring new things can be life changing. When you dip your toe in the pool of possibilities you never know what extraordinary things may occur — the universe may open a gateway to new experiences that align and resonate with your soul. Allow your intuition to guide you as you explore what calls to you. When presented with an opportunity, ask yourself if it is right for you. Of course, you can ask your friends and family for advice, but consider whether they are responding with your best interests in mind. More importantly, do they know what's in your heart and mind? Only you know that.

This wisdom guided my own journey when I felt called to become a yoga teacher. Becoming a yoga teacher was incredibly hard work, but the journey helped me transform both physically and mentally. I recognized that my body was strong and capable of doing this training, even after being told that I might have limitations due to the intensive TRAM-flap breast reconstructive surgery that I had six years prior. But I knew this decision was another important step on the spiritual path I was on. I was already a Reiki Master and teacher; becoming a yoga instructor was another role in alignment with my purpose.

But as I mentioned earlier, it did come with feelings of imposter syndrome, which can be particularly loud during times of reinvention, planting seeds of doubt within our minds. Imposter syndrome sounds like these thoughts that I had before I started teaching yoga such as: "Who am I to think that I could teach a class? What are people going to think? Are people even going to show up? Will they know when I mess up?" That voice of fear can be exhausting. When it shows up for you, put it in its place. Claim your worth and don't let fear get in the way of pursuing what calls to you.

When I started teaching, I was nervous before each class but once I stepped onto that mat, I stepped into the role that I knew was meant for me and had been training for most of my life. Suddenly it didn't matter that I was fifty-five and just starting out as a teacher. I had years of experience as a student, and I could relate to where people were in their lives — from moms to Empresses. I wanted to inspire women of all ages to begin a practice of yoga because I knew how life-changing it could be. Today, I continue to learn and try new things, deepening my practice by extensively studying qigong — another transformative energy practice that I now teach alongside yoga — podcasting, and writing this book. Every new chapter proves that it's never too late to become who you're meant to be.

An Empress recognizes her sovereignty through her choices. You can sit around and tell yourself that you're too old to start something new, or you can begin creating a new future. You can replace self-doubt with daily affirmations of your wisdom and worth. You can leave a long career to pursue work that feeds your soul. You can finally write that book that only you can write. You can discard outdated clothes and create a new style. You can choose not to wear makeup or dye your hair purple simply because you want to. You are empowered to make the choices that best suit you.

There have been many women who have done remarkable things in their Empress years. Everything from publishing bestsellers, completing marathons, winning Oscars for the first time, and becoming successful entrepreneurs. We have so much to offer. We are not defined by our age, and we certainly shouldn't let it stop us from enjoying more intimate relationships, professional and creative endeavors, adventure and exploration, digital empowerment, and renewed vitality.

Imagine you're stepping into a new kingdom of opportunities where fear and self-limiting beliefs no longer block your path. Fear and self-doubt are invisible barriers that prevent you from trying new things and diminish your natural spontaneity. Ask yourself what is holding you back from living your life on purpose. Whether it's learning something new or letting go of something that doesn't serve your greatest and highest good, you have the power to make the changes you desire.

Find something that ignites your passion and take small steps toward it. Reinvention in your Empress years isn't about proving anything to anyone else — it's about listening to your own wisdom, that inner voice that is encouraging you to live your life to the fullest. After all, an Empress never stops expanding her kingdom.

YOUR ROYAL INVITATION

REFLECTION JOURNAL PROMPTS

Below are a few questions to ask yourself as you embrace reinvention. You can choose to write about these in your journal. Be honest while trying not to overthink it. Usually, the first thing that pops up in your mind is inspired by your truest self.

- What dreams have I set aside that still whisper to me?
- What new experiences are calling to me?
- What am I passionate about?
- What self-limiting beliefs about my age or abilities am I ready to release?
- When I envision myself in five years, what am I doing?
- What specific fears arise when I think about making significant changes?
- When I contemplate reinvention, what sensations do I notice in my body?
- What patterns have kept me from reinventing myself in the past? How might I approach things differently now?
- Who in my life would support me as I reinvent myself?
- What does success in this reinvention look and feel like for me?

DAILY PRACTICE

Use the following affirmations to support your reinvention journey. Choose one that resonates with your current challenge or practice them all as a complete ritual.

FOR AWAKENING CURIOSITY

Place your hand on your heart each morning and say:

Today I invite curiosity into my life. I will notice what sparks my interest and follow that spark, even if it's just for a moment.

FOR FACING FEAR

When you feel fear arising as you consider a new path, place your hands on your heart and say:

I invite courage to walk beside me as I step into the unknown. My Empress energy is stronger than my fear.

FOR RELEASING AGE LIMITATIONS

When you hear yourself saying that you're too old or that it's too late to start something new, place both hands on your heart and say:

I grant myself permission to begin anew regardless of my age. Time is my ally, not my enemy.

FOR ACCESSING WISDOM

When facing a challenge in your reinvention journey, place your hands on your solar plexus and say:

I invite my deep wisdom to guide me. The answers I seek are already within me.

FOR FINDING COMMUNITY

When feeling isolated in your journey, open your arms wide and say:

I invite connection with other Empresses who are also reinventing themselves. Our collective wisdom strengthens my own path.

FOR CELEBRATING PROGRESS

Each time you take a step forward discovering what lights you up, raise your hands and declare:

I celebrate this courageous Empress who continues to evolve.

New Moon Ritual for Setting Intentions

The New Moon is a great time to plant seeds for reinvention or new beginnings, and this is a simple ritual that you can perform each month. It is a way to set your intentions or wishes on what you would like to manifest. Trust that the universe will provide what is for your greatest and highest good. You can do a full ceremony or keep it simple. Find what resonates with you.

Setting Your Sacred Space: Gather a few simple elements to enhance this ritual:

- A candle (white or any color that feels right to you)
- Your Empress journal and a pen
- Crystals or other objects that you would like to place on your alter.

Go to your throne or sacred space where you can be undisturbed.

1. Begin by clearing the energy in your chosen space. You can open a window or just set the intention that you're clearing the space.

2. Create an altar with your objects, placing them in any way that seems appropriate. You can invite in other objects that resonate with you.

3. Light your candle.

4. Sit comfortably and take three deep breaths.

5. Place your hands on your heart and say, "I enter this sacred moment as the Empress of my life. I am wise, I am experienced, I am powerful. I am ready to discover what truly ignites my spirit"

6. If you already have a new direction in mind, you can focus on it while repeating a modified version: "I enter this

sacred moment as the Empress of my life. I am wise, I am experienced, I am powerful. I am ready to embark on this new journey."

7. In your journal, write down what you wish to manifest under the energies of the new moon. You can begin each sentence with "I wish to..." or "I want..." List as many as you'd like.

8. Once you are done, close the journal and say, "I now release this to the energy of the New Moon. I trust in the guidance of the universe and all there is for my greatest and highest good."

9. Extinguish the candle.

CHAPTER 14

THE SOVEREIGN POWER OF FORGIVENESS: WHEN AN EMPRESS FINDS HER FREEDOM

An Empress understands the sovereign power of forgiveness. She recognizes this act not as a weakness, but as liberation — a conscious choice to reclaim her energy and free herself from energetic bonds that no longer serve her. Through this sacred practice, she heals her own wounds and transforms her relationships with others. In choosing forgiveness, she refuses to remain a prisoner of someone else's action.

Forgiveness holds extraordinary healing powers that extend across all dimensions of being —physical, emotional, spiritual, and energetic. When an Empress chooses this path, she makes a deliberate decision about where her precious energy flows.

When you choose not to forgive, you remain energetically tethered to the very person who caused you pain — an invisible but powerful cord binding you to experiences you wish to release. I invite you to examine what you're holding onto and ask: Is this serving my highest purpose? Do I want an energetic cord keeping me bound to past situations, or do I wish to feel liberated from these ties? This is the sovereign power of forgiveness — the ability to cut the cords that bind you to what no longer serves.

Forgiving someone who has hurt you is rarely easy. Their actions may have left deep emotional scars, yet without forgiveness these wounds cannot truly heal. When you withhold forgiveness, you create an energetic connection that dims your internal light and becomes an anchor weighing you down. The path to freedom lies in letting go. Through forgiveness, you sever the cord tying you to that person or situation, releasing the stuck energy within your system. Once you cut this connection, the feeling of heaviness dissolves, and you reclaim your sovereign power. You'll feel lighter, having released their hold on you, allowing yourself to move forward and shine fully once again.

Throughout my journey, I've encountered moments when severing energetic connections became necessary for my well-being. One such bond wasn't merely a cord — it was more like a thick chain connecting me to a former partner. This energetic restraint was silently sabotaging my heart's capacity to open fully. I discovered it was preventing me from attracting and nurturing healthy romantic connections. I built protective walls around my heart as a way of keeping others at a distance. What I was doing was preventing myself from allowing deeper love from flowing.

During a series of meditation sessions, I journeyed inward seeking guidance about what was blocking me from experiencing relationships I truly deserved. The answer revealed itself with clarity: In my mind's eye appeared a thick chain anchoring me to a past relationship. I felt old wounds beginning to reopen, my heart responding with a familiar ache that had never fully healed. In that moment, I remembered a passage from a book that said that the very act of forgiveness can melt the icicles around a person's heart, allowing them to love again. I understood what I needed to do to sever the energetic binds.

What I did next would help dissolve the chain. I visualized us standing in the same room with this cord connecting us as I sent forgiveness through it. I imagined myself saying it out loud as the cord started to glow with white light, sending the energy of release to the other person. I told him that I forgive everything that he did to cause pain and suffering and that I no longer needed to be connected to his energy. After a few moments, I imagined taking a chain cutter and severing the connection. Once I did that, the chain floated away, and he dissolved into a million pieces like dust in the wind.

As the visualization completed, I didn't realize I had been holding my breath until I let out a big sigh of relief. The sensation was immediate. I felt lighter, as if a physical weight had been lifted from my chest, allowing me to breathe deeper than I had in years. All the time that had passed between the relationship's end and this moment of forgiveness, I had been imprisoned behind that chain. It wasn't until I fully embraced forgiveness that I truly freed myself, reclaiming my heart and my personal power.

Forgiveness doesn't require a conversation, confrontation, or the other person's awareness to be effective. When you forgive someone, you release the energy around that person and what they did to you. You can send a message of forgiveness from yourself to their higher self. Your higher self is that part of your spirit that is loving and kind and doesn't judge. It refers to a more evolved, aware, and enlightened aspect of your consciousness that transcends ego. You have a higher self that you can connect to through meditation or when you're in a creative flow state, or retreating to your inner throne. When you send that message of forgiveness, you are essentially transmuting the energy and are releasing the hold that it has on you.

This energetic clearing is essential for your physical well-being too. When you repress emotions like anger or sadness, it affects the chakras or energetic system in the body and can create disease. Traditional Chinese Medicine and meridian theory also teach us this principle. Your body has channels of energy flowing to and from your organs. Each organ is associated with specific emotions. For example, anger is associated with the liver, fear with the kidneys, worry with the stomach, joy with the heart, and grief with the lungs.

Forgiveness directly impacts this emotional-physical balance. When you withhold forgiveness, you may experience multiple emotional experiences simultaneously — frustration and anger toward the person who hurt you, sadness about the painful situation, and grief over what might have been. Unresolved emotional pain can create imbalances in your body and manifest as physical issues.

You can also forgive someone who has passed away. Within my personal and ongoing spiritual journey, I discovered that I had some inner child wounds to explore. I felt that some of my struggles were linked to the relationship that I'd had with my mom. There has been much written on the topic of shadow work, finding parts of yourself that are repressed and need to surface to address and release. I realized that I needed to forgive her for some of the ways I was treated. Although this was difficult, it was an important part of my healing.

My mom was a loving and beautiful person who struggled with anger, becoming frustrated when things weren't done her way. She had ensured a difficult childhood marked by physical and emotional abuse, which likely shaped how she managed emotions. She also suffered from epilepsy — a neurological condition that possibly affected her behavior — during an era when mental health was rarely discussed openly. As a child, I learned to navigate our relationship by recognizing her triggers, though we never spoke about them directly. Despite her challenges, I understood she carried her own suffering.

I realize that healing myself requires healing my relationship with my mother, even though she had passed years before. Fortunately, I've always felt connected to the spiritual realm, sensing the presence of loved ones who have crossed over. This gift allows me to converse with her spirit — conversations that become a powerful gateway to healing. Through these spiritual dialogues, we are building the relationship we couldn't fully achieve during her earthly life. I believe that symbols carry messages and spirit often finds ways to show them to us. I often notice the number 127 (my birthday) appearing repeatedly on clocks and on my phone. This isn't a coincidence; it's her gentle signature, a reassurance that she remains close.

Sometimes the person most in need of our forgiveness is the one who stares back at us in the mirror. After walking this earth for many seasons, each of us carries memories of moments when we fell short of our ideals, times when our actions contributed to situations that served no one's highest good. When these memories weigh on our hearts, self-forgiveness becomes a necessary medicine. While we cannot rewrite the past, we can transmute the energy surrounding it through the act of forgiving ourselves. In this sacred space of self-compassion, we can extend the same grace and understanding to ourselves that we so readily offer others.

Through self-forgiveness, we release the energetic hold these situations maintain over us. Rather than truly forgetting, we free ourselves from the emotional burden while retaining the wisdom our experiences have taught us. The word "forgiveness" itself reveals this truth — it is literally "for-giving," a gift we can bestow upon others and, perhaps most importantly, upon ourselves.

When an Empress practices forgiveness, she doesn't do so merely for others — she does so because it liberates her spirit and allows her to rule with grace, wisdom, and power. Through forgiveness, she releases the past's hold on her present, creating space for new blessings to enter her royal court. Remember: Forgiveness is not forgetting. It is rising above, seeing with compassionate clarity, and choosing sovereignty over suffering. This is the Empress's way.

YOUR ROYAL INVITATION

This guided visualization will help you release energetic bonds and while honoring both your pain and your power to heal.

A Powerful Forgiveness Ritual

Begin by finding a comfortable seated position and placing your feet firmly on the ground. Feel your connection to the earth's supportive energy beneath you. Close your eyes and take three cleansing breaths.

Set a clear intention for this healing work by silently saying: "I am ready to release what no longer serves me and reclaim my sovereign power."

Imagine a beautiful pink light coming into your lotus crown and into your heart. Pink represents compassion and forgiveness. Feel this gentle, healing light swirling and expanding in your heart chakra.

When you are ready, think about someone you need to forgive. See them in your mind's eye in whatever image appears naturally. If visualizing them feels difficult, simply imagine their silhouette or outline.

If emotions arise, allow them to surface without judgement. Use your exhale to gently release any tension or discomfort you feel.

Now, visualize an energetic cord connecting your heart to theirs. Notice the quality of this cord — it's color, texture and density. This represents the energetic bond that has kept you tied to this person and situation.

See the pink light from your heart beginning to flow along this cord toward the other person. As the light reaches them, repeat this phrase three times with intention: "I release you through forgiveness."

Watch as the pink light begins to dissolve the cord completely, breaking it apart until it floats away like stardust, no longer connecting you to this person's energy.

Now, place both hands over your heart and feel the pink light flowing throughout your entire being. Offer yourself loving words that heal the wounded aspects of your spirit. Say aloud or silently: "I love myself completely" or "I heal aspects of myself that experienced pain," or whatever sovereign words arise from your heart.

You may experience sudden emotions or even shed tears. You are healing; honor what shows up.

Continue to feel this beautiful, compassionate energy flow within you, dissolving old emotions of anger and hurt, replacing them with feelings of love and liberation.

Visualize a protective golden bubble surrounding your entire being, sealing your energy with radiant light.

Take a moment to express gratitude to yourself for having the courage to do this sacred work.

When you are ready, slowly open your eyes. Allow yourself time to rest and integrate this powerful transformation.

You can journal about your experience or simply sit in quiet appreciation of the healing you've just created.

CHAPTER 15

FROM NURTURING OTHERS TO NURTURING SELF: PRIORITIZING SELF-CARE

All the chapters in this book represent elements of self-care that an Empress can choose to integrate into her life. Self-care is essential to maintaining physical, emotional, and spiritual well-being. When we are busy taking care of our kingdom — the people we love, our work, and all the responsibilities we have — we can easily neglect to take care of the most important element: ourselves.

Women have always had to balance myriad demands, and sometimes they expand outside the intimate boundaries of one's hearth. We think that we have enough fuel to tend all the fires but neglect to nurture the flame that resides within ourselves. That flame is analogous to our personal health, well-being, and energy. When we don't tend our inner fire, it begins to die down and doesn't nourish all aspects of ourselves — the physical, emotional, spiritual, and energetic. We don't have enough energy to give to anyone.

When that happens, we may begin to experience symptoms of burn out, chronic exhaustion, insomnia, muscle tension, and other health issues. Our nervous system becomes dysregulated as we manage the energy of fight, flight, and frenzy. Sometimes, we may not even realize how far we've pushed ourselves until we are lying flat on the couch, exhausted. It is important for an Empress to place her own needs above others so that she has plenty of physical and mental capacity to assist others without feeling fully depleted.

As a yoga and qigong instructor, I have studied how the body's nervous system can suffer if we aren't attuned to what's happening within us and restore harmony to our internal state. Our nervous system can become dysregulated for various reasons, including chronic stress, trauma, substance abuse, and hormonal fluctuations. In an extreme state of trauma, people suffer from stress disorders that disconnect them from bodily sensations until something triggers their awareness. This can manifest as heightened sensitivity to our surroundings and episodes of intense anxiety. Have you ever experienced a panic attack or something close to that? When your system becomes overwhelmed this way, you must find your center again through soothing practices, like deep-breathing exercises, a warm bath, gentle restorative yoga, or grounding meditations or techniques. A regular ritual of self-care is important to help safeguard our kingdom. Our mental and physical states deserve to be taken care of.

My children were young when I was first diagnosed with breast cancer. Not only was I a full-time mom, but as a realtor, I was putting clients' needs ahead of mine. I was running on fumes. I ignored the warning signs or was too tired to see them, and my body responded. Breast cancer was my wake-up call.

After my diagnosis, I began exploring the deeper connections between our emotional patterns and physical health. Louise Hay wrote a book called Heal Your Body: The Mental Causes for Physical Illness and the Metaphysical Ways to Heal Them, and I remember looking up the "spiritual" reason behind breast cancer in this book and it made so much sense. She wrote that breast problems occurred because we put everyone else's needs first. We nourish others before we nourish ourselves. Sometimes we neglect our own needs. That is probably true of every woman who has had any type of physical challenge associated with her breasts or her womb. We have a hard time saying no because we feel we need to do it all and that we can do it best.

Do you often say yes to something when you really want to say no? Do you neglect self-care but are always the first one to help others? Women generally consider nurturing and caregiving to be part of our identity, deeply ingrained in our nature. We take care of others because it's what we do and know. I'm not suggesting you stop doing this, I'm encouraging you to become more aware of when you are running out of energy. Pay attention to the physical sensations in your body — the tension in your lower back or the stiffness in your shoulders that indicate you are out of balance. Notice when you look in the mirror and see that you appear less vibrant, or when you feel less radiant and energetic. Pay attention to the signs telling you the scale has tipped and you're out of balance.

When I teach qigong, I emphasize the importance of yin and yang energy in maintaining harmony and balance within our energy. We all possess both forms of energy. Yang is masculine energy — the fire within us that drives us forward and fuels our actions. On the other hand, yin is feminine energy — the nurturing, restorative quality that allows us to receive and restore. When we have an excess of yang energy and not enough yin energy, we are out of balance. It is our responsibility to nurture and tend to our inner fire, recognizing the imbalance and restoring it to homeostasis — a state of balance within the body's systems that are needed for proper functioning.

This delicate balance becomes even more crucial during the transitions of our Empress years. As we age and our children leave the nest, new responsibilities often emerge. You might find yourself caring for grandchildren — a role that brings extreme joy but also demands significant life force energy. Taking care of a child in your twenties or thirties is different than when you're in your Empress years. Many of us find ourselves caring for elderly parents, requiring even more of our energetic resources. While you may enjoy these roles, maintaining your own energy balance requires prioritizing self-care first. Remember, you need to fill your cup before you can share it with others.

It's crucial to identify activities that bring you a sense of renewal. Whether it's a leisurely stroll in nature, reading time, or a relaxing cup of tea, planning these activities is essential. They serve as reminders, both to you and others, that you are valuable and your personal resources are precious.

It is equally important to maintain the proper doctor visits good eating and sleeping habits. I have spoken to countless women who have neglected their personal care and not visited their doctors for

annual physicals or gynecological exams only to discover an underlying condition that could have been prevented or treated early.
We cannot neglect our bodies. We owe it to ourselves to get regular
checkups, even if they feel uncomfortable or produce some anxiety.
Why neglect the opportunity to empower your well-being by taking
the appropriate self-care steps? You're empowered to be your own
advocate. Step into that space with authority.

I am diligent about scheduling my yearly doctor appointments:
a physical, an eye exam, skin checks, breast care and a gynecologist
appointment – all the essential preventative care visits. I know that if I
do, there is a chance that an underlying condition will be caught early.
At one of my gynecologist appointments, my pap smear showed some
cell activity that looked suspicious. Extra tests, pelvic ultrasounds, and
a biopsy of my uterus were performed. Luckily, the results were normal, but I was nervous the entire time I was waiting for the results.

My body was physically drained and my mind active. I understood what I had to do — rest — even though it was incredibly challenging for me. I knew that was what my body needed. I sat on the
couch and watched some feel-good shows, I read, I drank nourishing
tea, and I took care of myself. I told myself that no matter what happened, I would be prepared to handle it.

I try not to give my power away to excessive worry, though we
all worry, or to feeling like a victim, though that emotion sneaks in
too. We can try our best to stay positive and use hope as fuel to help
us through those times when we're waiting for results or waiting for
treatments. We can pray or get a Reiki session or do some breathwork to calm us. Calling upon our spirit guides, angels or higher self
can also help you. Tune in and ask yourself what you need in this
moment or for guidance on navigating a certain situation. Then listen for the answer.

Ever since my breast reconstructive surgery, I have also learned
to love and honor my body. Instead of feeling badly or sorry for myself, I have learned to embrace the new me. When I look in the mirror, I am reminded of the warrior that I am and the path that I'm on
to survive with the utmost love and compassion for myself. Within
the recipe of self-care is also remaining in a state of positivity and
hope, which are critical components to nurturing our soul.

Over the years I have changed many lifestyle behaviors. I take better care of myself physically and mentally, and I'm always making adjustments. A few years ago, I stopped drinking alcohol, and it was one of the best decisions that I've ever made. I thought about the consequences of long-term drinking — diminished health, increased inflammation, joint pain, and so forth. I felt empowered to take control of the habit of drinking and eliminate it from my life because I knew that it was the best thing to do for my long-term health. It wasn't easy, so I joined a program that showed scientific evidence about the effects of alcohol and helped individuals stop drinking through coaching, educational videos and habit-changing exercises. I also did very specific qigong exercises and self-Reiki practices to shift my energy and break old patterns. All of these helped me to become alcohol free.

I recently decided to see a functional medicine doctor who tested for far more than the standard cholesterol and vitamin D3. Through comprehensive bloodwork, she tested for food allergies and inflammation markers. I was shocked to learn I was allergic to several foods I'd been eating for years!

She also tested my microbiome, which is now considered our second brain since its health affects everything in our body. The results revealed I had leaky gut from years of taking acetaminophen, antibiotics, and eating gluten. I now follow a specific supplement protocol and nutritional plan to heal these imbalances.

Knowing that my years of drinking alcohol and certain dietary choices had created inflammation — and that inflammation can contribute to cancer, which I've already battled — was motivation enough to change my lifestyle completely. This experience taught me that being proactive about our health pays off. We don't have to accept feeling unwell as normal. When we identify what's affecting our health, find proper care, and make the appropriate lifestyle adjustments, we give ourselves the best chance of living healthier lives.

I maintain a regular movement practice like yoga, qigong, and walking because I want to have strength and balance in my body as I age. The less we do, the weaker our muscles and bones become. This becomes even more important as we get older, while maintaining mobility and preventing falls becomes crucial. By doing our part and prioritizing self-care we are telling ourselves that we are worthy and deserving of care.

Today, we have many resources that can help us. There are natural products, functional doctors and holistic practitioners. We also have access to countless books covering everything from mental health and hormonal balance to nutrition and holistic wellness — topics that were rarely discussed openly in previous generations. In addition, more women are writing about these topics and offering their expertise and guidance for Empresses like us. We have more female doctors who understand the changing physical and emotional landscapes of a woman's life. And we have an abundance of online videos for any type of movement practice you can imagine — from gentle yoga to energizing belly dancing!

Besides taking care of your physical body, you need to feel stable and supported within your own personal kingdom. Your social network plays a crucial role in your self-care foundation. Do you have a tribe that allows you to show up as your most authentic self without judgment? Are you comfortable expressing yourself and speaking your truth? Do you have someone who actively listens when you need to be heard? Can you ask for help when you need it, and do you have resources to offer help in return? If not, actively seek out those you can support and create a healthy exchange of energy.

Finally, reflect on your relationship with your inner voice. Is your internal dialogue supportive and compassionate, or do you find yourself engaged in self-criticism? Notice how you speak to yourself when you make mistakes or face a challenge. An Empress recognizes that her inner throne should be filled with wisdom and kindness, not judgement and self-doubt. Consider whether you treat yourself with the same grace and kindness that you extend to those you love. That inner voice can affect your mental health and how you cope with things. Practices like meditation or working with a mental health professional can help transform your inner landscape into one that nurtures rather than diminishes your spirit. These questions will help you identify gaps within your kingdom that may need your royal attention.

Once you've identified these gaps or imbalances in your life, the next step is taking appropriate action. When you're overcome with exhaustion, gentle qigong movement can restore energy. When you're trapped in mental spirals, expressing and releasing those thoughts becomes essential. When illness arises, seeking answers becomes the priority. You must address these imbalances before they grow beyond your control, making ongoing self-care a lifelong commitment. An Empress may appear strong and self-sufficient, but that doesn't mean she doesn't experience moments of isolation or feel hesitant to seek help or voice her needs. She deserves to be both seen and heard in her vulnerability.

Cultivating strength in spirit leads to strength in body and mind. I've seen many women take ownership of their health, even after a life-altering diagnosis, only to discover reservoirs of courage and resilience they never knew they possessed. Some have gone on to help other women who are having similar struggles. Their voice and resilience have become a superpower. But self-care can be anyone's superpower, and it should be every Empress's. Claim this practice as the cornerstone of your sovereignty — a well-nourished Empress transforms not only her life but the lives of all she touches.

YOUR ROYAL INVITATION

Here are some practical ways to incorporate more self-care into your daily life:

- **Schedule it intentionally.** Block out time in your calendar specifically for self-care activities, giving them the same priority as other appointments.

- **Use a wellness tracker:** Make a list of all the necessary doctor appointments —gynecologist, vision care, dermatologist, annual physical, regular dental cleanings and any others. Write down the dates of your previous and future appointments.

- **Start small.** Begin with just five or ten minutes devoted to self-care daily rather than trying to implement drastic changes at once.

- **Identify what genuinely recharges you.** Self-care looks different for everyone. Reflect on activities that truly make you feel restored rather than following trends.

- **Set boundaries.** Practice saying no to additional responsibilities when your plate is full. Boundaries protect your time and energy.

- **Connect meaningfully.** Nurture relationships that are supportive and positive; consider limiting time with people who drain your energy.

- **Prioritize rest.** Ensure you're getting adequate sleep and incorporate moments of rest throughout your day.

- **Engage in movement that feels good.** Find physical activities you genuinely enjoy rather than exercising solely for appearance-related goals.

- **Create morning and evening rituals.** Bookend your days with small practices that ground you and create transition moments.

- **Reduce digital consumption.** Set limits on social media and news intake, which both deplete mental energy.

- **Practice self-compassion.** Speak to yourself with the same kindness you would offer a good friend.

CHAPTER 16

THE EMPRESS'S BOUNTY: LIVING IN ABUNDANCE AND GRATITUDE

In this chapter, we explore the twin pillars that form the foundation of an Empress's rich and fulfilling life: abundance and gratitude. These complementary forces create a powerful cycle of receiving and appreciating that enriches every aspect of your kingdom. When you understand how to cultivate a mindset of abundance and develop the practice of heartfelt gratitude, you transform not only what you receive but how deeply you experience each gift that comes your way.

Cultivating an Abundance Mindset

An Empress sits on her throne, radiating gratitude for the abundance flowing through her life. Surrounded by love, family, friends, and her thriving kingdom, she basks in all she has manifested. Through conscious choices, she continues to invite harmony and balance into her realm.

The Empress archetype in tarot embodies abundance, fertility, femininity, beauty, and connection to nature. From her throne, she savors all she has manifested and all the universe generously offers. Her fertility extends beyond the physical; she plants seeds for meaningful endeavors that enrich her life and kingdom. As a wisdom-keeper, she guides others with her hard-won insights. She stands empowered, content, and profoundly grateful for everything she possesses and for every experience — both gentle and challenging — that has shaped her journey.

The Empress whispers, "The universe is infinitely bountiful. Open your arms wide to receive its gifts." True abundance transcends material wealth. It encompasses love, vibrant health, wisdom, meaningful experiences, and limitless opportunities. When you shift your perspective from scarcity to abundance, you begin to recognize the multifaceted richness already present in your life. When you deeply feel that you have enough and are worthy, the universe discovers even more ways to provide for you. Honor each accomplishment along your journey, whether seemingly insignificant or monumental. Celebrate every fruit of your labor. Each one deserves recognition.

Yet, for many of us, embracing this abundant perspective doesn't come naturally. Our relationship with abundance is often complicated by deeply ingrained patterns of scarcity thinking. When you have a scarcity mindset, you will never feel as if you have enough — not enough love, capability or intelligence. This drives you to exhaust yourself seeking external validation. You might continuously please others only to feel unappreciated and taken for granted. Perhaps beneath these feelings lies a sense of unworthiness or, more painfully, an absence of self-love. Have you ever experienced this? Have you felt the world's weight pressing down on your shoulders and at the same time not feeling that the universe has your back?

The moment we genuinely feel worthy of receiving abundance — worthy of manifesting our deepest desires — the world unfolds and delivers precisely what we need. We may not always receive exactly what we want in the exact form we envision, but we will receive what serves our highest purpose and greatest good.

The difference between achieving your goals and creating extraordinary life experiences lies in your mindset. When morning comes, do you dread the day ahead? Are you already convincing yourself it won't be wonderful? Remember that words and thoughts have energy and what you believe becomes your reality. The wisdom of "energy flows where the intention goes" reminds us that your beliefs have a profound impact on your reality. If you believe in something, whether, positive or negative, then it will manifest in your life. By shifting your perspective, you can transform the energy surrounding your experiences.

So how do we begin this essential mindset transformation? Transforming your mindset requires more than repeating affirmations though this practice provides a foundation. Become attentive to what arises within you. Notice the specific phrases and thoughts that appear when you awaken or when your mind begins its familiar patterns. Recognizing these repetitive thought patterns marks the beginning of your transformation. This awareness allows you to "flip the script" — actively changing the inner dialogue and reshaping your perspective. This process requires effort and consistent awareness, but it becomes increasingly natural with practice. Your emotional state will improve. Positive energy will gravitate toward you, and manifesting your aspirations will become more effortless and joyful.

As you cultivate this transformed mindset, you'll discover that abundance itself takes on a more expansive and personal meaning. Abundance means something different to everyone. You can feel abundance in your love life when you lovingly connect to a partner, in your social life when you are surrounded by friends who celebrate your victories. You might experience it in your creative life when ideas flow freely like a spiritually guided brush on a canvas, and in how it pertains to your financial stability when you feel secure in your resources. An Empress recognizes abundance in her wisdom and in the life experiences that shaped it, and in her ability to inspire others. She knows that abundance can be discovered in the small gifts that life provides, like a beautiful sunset. You define what abundance means to you. It might be a peaceful morning while writing in your journal, or time spent with your children, grandchildren, or pets. Abundance can also be found in the satisfaction of mentoring other women on their path. How do you define abundance in your life?

As a single woman with a mortgage, bills, and my beloved dog, I shouldered complete responsibility for my financial security during my time as a consultant. The unpredictable nature of consulting meant assignments could end unexpectedly — and that happened when one company completed their system implementation and depleted their consulting budget, leaving me to find a new job. Despite having some savings, I knew I needed to secure another position quickly.

Rather than panic or slip into scarcity thinking, I chose to trust in abundance and take inspired action. I called job recruiters, informed them of my availability and asked them to notify me when opportunities arose. Each morning, I wrote in my journal: "I will find the perfect assignment for my highest good, one that matches my skills and meets my financial needs." After several months, an friend and former colleague called about an opportunity perfectly suited to my skills and expertise in a company in New Jersey, conveniently within my home state. After meeting with the project and department managers, I secured the position. This job brought an unexpected blessing: meeting my husband on my very first day. I recall our first handshake vividly; I literally felt energy coursing through my palms. Was this the universe signaling something magical? Though we didn't begin dating until eight months later as the project concluded, we've now shared over twenty wonderful years together and two beautiful children.

This experience taught me a lesson about the relationship between intention and manifesting. Where our attention or intention goes, our energy will follow. I'm not saying you simply state your intention and passively wait. You must actively develop your skills, nurture your connections, and identify and address your limiting beliefs. When you've prepared yourself fully, abundance naturally flows into your life. Gratitude forms the essential foundation of abundance awareness. When you sincerely appreciate what you already possess, it serves as a key to unlocking doors to receiving even more. This appreciation isn't about comparison or competition — it's about recognizing the richness already present in your life. As you cultivate this grateful awareness, you discover that abundance and gratitude form a partnership, each strengthening the other in a beautiful, continuous cycle. This transforms not only how you perceive your world but how you experience every moment within it.

The Art of Gratitude

Gratitude is the art of feeling truly thankful, a practice of developing a keen awareness of the gifts in our lives, both magnificent and mundane. When we practice gratitude, we anchor ourselves in the present moment, releasing worries about the past or anxieties about the future. Gratitude teaches us that perfection isn't the goal, and that beauty often resides within the imperfections themselves. This practice manifests not just in our minds, but in our very bodies. Gratitude flows directly from the heart. Watch someone experiencing profound gratitude, and you'll often see them instinctively place their hands over their heart. The emotion runs so deep that it sometimes transcends words, leaving us momentarily speechless in its presence.

This physical expression reveals a deeper truth: gratitude is fundamentally about recognizing value. It stands in direct opposition to taking things for granted. When we take something for granted, we fail to acknowledge its significance — it's simply "there." The nourishing food on our table, the supportive people in our lives, the shelter that protects us, all deserve our recognition because they greatly enrich our existence. This recognition of value shapes my daily practice. Each morning when I awaken, I feel grateful for the gift of another day on this magnificent earth. I don't list out every blessing, but I intentionally cultivate gratitude throughout my day as a gentle reminder to treasure everything and everyone in my life.

Since I began my spiritual journey, I have noticed more books supporting the topic of gratitude, and for good reason. Years ago, while struggling with chronic pain and fighting to maintain a positive mindset, I discovered a simple, yet powerful suggestion that transformed my life: take a moment at day's end to write down three things you're grateful for. As someone who loves beautiful journals, this practice gave me the perfect excuse to purchase a special one dedicated solely to gratitude. Each night, I would record three moments from the day, sometimes as simple as "I savored a delicious lunch," or "I made someone laugh today." This ritual became something I looked forward to, a sacred pause that allowed me to reflect and savor the day's gifts. Often, I found myself writing more than three entries. I always drifted to sleep with a heart full of appreciation.

Over time, I noticed remarkable changes. My mental outlook brightened. My physical body relaxed. Life seemed richer, more vibrant. Opportunities began appearing more frequently, as if gratitude had opened new channels for abundance to flow. On days when I wasn't feeling my best, that veil would lift, revealing more contentment. My perspective shifted throughout each day as I began to recognize moments worthy of gratitude: an easy commute, uplifting songs on the radio that inspired spontaneous car singing, a stranger holding a door, or that perfect first sip of morning coffee. We can find things everywhere to be grateful for, and we don't have to look hard. Through this practice, I discovered that gratitude is an art — one that we can transform the way we see the world.

How Gratitude Transforms Us

As an Empress who has weathered life's storms and emerged stronger, I've discovered that gratitude is perhaps our most powerful alchemical tool. It transforms not just our circumstances but our very essence. Through years of practice, I've witnessed how gratitude rewrites our internal narrative, turning scarcity into abundance, fear into courage, and isolation into connection. When we cultivate this sacred practice, we don't merely survive our challenges, we convert them into wisdom. Gratitude anchors us in the present moment while simultaneously opening our hearts to receive life's endless gifts. This is the true magic of an Empress: She knows that gratitude is a sovereign choice that shapes her entire kingdom.

During times of stress or panic, gratitude emerges as a powerful solution. By reflecting on the challenges you've already overcome and acknowledging the abundance in your life, you find reassurance when you need it most. Expressing gratitude outwardly is as essential as feeling it inwardly. What better way to honor someone than by thanking them or letting them know you appreciate them just for their presence? These expressions release happiness hormones for both the giver and receiver. When we speak the words "thank you" or "I appreciate you," we create soft, uplifting energy vibrations through our throat chakra. Words carry energy, and gratitude-filled expressions elevate our internal vibration.

Gratitude directly influences our heart chakra as well. Remember the Grinch from How the Grinch Stole Christmas? By the story's end, gratitude had completely transformed him. His heart expanded beyond its previous limitations, fundamentally changing his energy and his entire being. This fictional example illustrates that gratitude has the power to transform us at our very core, expanding our capacity for love and connection.

When navigating difficult circumstances, seeing anything deserving of appreciation can seem impossible. Often, I've only recognized the benefits of challenging situations in retrospect. My past relationships taught me resilience, resourcefulness, greater self-awareness, and self-compassion. They helped me prioritize my needs rather than constantly addressing others' needs for validation. I now feel genuinely grateful for the growth these difficult partnerships inspired.

In my early thirties, I became completely absorbed in a toxic relationship with someone emotionally abusive, though I couldn't recognize those patterns at the time. I remained unaware of how mistreated and emotionally depleted I had become. He didn't want children, and I convinced myself to abandon a core desire to have my own. When he ended the relationship without explanation, I was devastated and lost. Today, I recognize this painful ending as the universe's gift — a divine intervention that freed me to become the mother I was meant to be and step into my own power.

The journey that followed was challenging but transformative. Like a phoenix rising out of the ashes or like a caged bird finally spreading her wings, I discovered freedom in what initially felt like abandonment. This experience taught me never to sacrifice my core desires and revealed inner strength I didn't know I possessed. Beyond traditional therapy, I found healing and growth in spiritual practices. Through this process, I emerged stronger and more resilient.

Several months after the breakup, a business trip to Arizona led to an unexpected day trip to Sedona. My colleague insisted I visit this special place with its magical energy vortexes. This was the early 1990s before Sedona had fully emerged as the spiritual mecca it is today. Little did I know this visit would place me on a path of spiritual awakening.

The magnificent red rock formations and breathtaking scenery captivated me completely. After hiking some gentle trails, we stopped for lunch and shopping in the village of Tlaquepaque. I wandered into a shop filled with crystals, music, and books. Never had I seen such an extensive collection of spiritual and self-help literature. It was still all new to me and I was fascinated by it all. As I explored, running my fingers along book spines and browsing through pages, I felt the space's calming energy — as if I was being gently guided towards something I needed.

Here, I discovered one book that would become a cornerstone of my healing: *Living with Joy* by Sanaya Roman. The title resonated deeply because I desperately needed more joy in my life. After reading the book and completing its inner work exercises, I experienced a significant energy shift. I learned about connecting with my higher self and transforming my energy around situations and people. I discovered the healing power of journaling to release my deepest thoughts.

During that trip, I also visited the Chapel of the Holy Cross, a church nestled into the mountainside, where I experienced such peace and tranquility. Sitting there gazing through the impressive window, I felt a compassionate presence enveloping me like a reassuring hug, promising that everything would eventually be okay. Sedona's reputation for mystical transformation proved true in my experience. My visit marked the beginning of a transformative journey that ultimately revealed my purpose. This is the power of gratitude: It doesn't change our past, but it transforms the energy around it. By practicing gratitude, we embrace possibility, hope, and joy.

As you step more deeply into your Empress energy, let gratitude become a natural part of who you are. Notice how it opens your heart and draws more abundance into your life. The simple act of acknowledging life's blessings creates a positive energy that touches everything around you. This is your sovereign power — to transform your experience by changing how you see and receive what life offers.

YOUR ROYAL INVITATION

These practices invite you to recognize the abundance already flowing through your life and cultivate deeper gratitude for every blessing, creating a powerful cycle that transforms how you receive and experience life's gifts.

PRACTICES FOR CULTIVATING ABUNDANCE

Reflection Journal Prompts:

- What does abundance mean to you beyond material wealth?
- When in your life have you felt most abundant? What created that feeling?
- What scarcity thoughts show up most frequently for you?
- How do you typically respond when good things happen to others?

Ongoing Practices:
Explore your abundance definition. Write about times you've felt truly abundant in life, energy, or relationships.

Recognize unexpected gifts. List three to five unexpected gifts or opportunities that recently came your way. How did they enrich your life?

Visualize your ideal day. Describe your ideal day. What would you do, and how would these activities make you feel?

Reframe scarcity thoughts. When you notice scarcity thinking, write down why you feel you don't have enough. Then challenge this belief with a reframe.

Practice abundance visualization. Visualize abundance flowing into your life. Practice generosity with others, whether through time or expertise, to create the natural cycle of giving and receiving.

Affirm your worthiness. Trust that there is enough for everyone, including you, and that you are worthy.

DAILY GRATITUDE RITUALS

Reflection Journal Prompts:

- What unexpected kindness did you receive today?
- Identify something you're grateful for but rarely acknowledge or often take for granted.
- Reflect on a challenge that taught you something valuable.

Ongoing Practices:

Create a gratitude jar. Write moments of gratitude on small pieces of paper and collect them. When you need a reminder of life's richness, draw a note from the jar.

Heart-centered gratitude. Place your hands over your heart and feel grateful for being the living, breathing wonder that you are. Acknowledge that the world shines brighter because you're in it. Feel gratitude for the Empress that you are.

Begin a Gratitude Journal.

Purchase a special notebook dedicated to this regal ritual or create a section in your Empress journal. You can label the journal or section "Gratitude Journal" or "What I'm Grateful For."

You might begin by listing constants you're always grateful for — family, health, special relationships. Then daily — morning, midday, or evening — record three things you feel grateful for. They can be as simple as finding a beautiful scarf on sale or enjoying lunch with friends.

Maintain this practice daily to experience its full benefits. Soon you'll eagerly anticipate these moments of reflection, and throughout your day, you'll naturally notice potential gratitude list moments. Before long, your entire world will sparkle with newfound appreciation.

CHAPTER 17

THE EMPRESS'S ENERGY: PROTECTING YOUR MOST SACRED POSSESSION

As an Empress who has traveled countless paths and gathered wisdom through the seasons of life, you've discovered a profound truth: your energy is your most sacred possession. Within your sovereign domain, this energetic essence must be both fiercely protected and deeply honored.

Energy comes in various forms. You have physical, mental, emotional, social, and spiritual energy. Physical energy comes from food that nourishes you and provides the fuel that powers all bodily functions, from basic metabolism to vigorous movement; it is influenced by sleep, nutrition, hydration and regular movement. Mental energy enables your ability to think clearly, focus, and process information; it is influenced by sleep, nutrition, stress levels, and mental stimulation. Emotional energy allows you to process feelings, build resilience for challenges, and fully enjoy positive experiences; it is nurtured through self-awareness, healthy relationships, and emotional expression. Social energy powers your connections with others and is replenished through meaningful interactions as well as time spent alone. Your spiritual energy connects you to something greater than yourself and helps you find purpose and meaning in life; it is cultivated through practices like quiet reflection, time in nature, prayer, or whatever brings you a sense of inner peace and spiritual growth.

These various forms of energy are deeply interconnected, creating a delicate web within your sovereign being. When one dimension suffers, the others may feel the impact. Fatigue negatively affects both physical and mental performance. When you're depleted, you cannot think clearly and your body can't perform optimally. Additionally, emotional exhaustion — the state of feeling completely drained and overwhelmed by accumulated stress — may interfere with your ability to connect meaningfully with others. When we isolate ourselves, our emotional and even physical energy can suffer. All the practices I've shared throughout this book address these different energy dimensions. Whether it's connecting to spiritual energy through your lotus crown, caring for your physical kingdom, healing emotionally through forgiveness, or renewing mental energy through reinvention — each practice nurtures a vital aspect of your being.

Your energy is a precious resource that requires daily attention and care, much like a cherished garden that flourishes with proper tending. When I teach qigong — a practice to cultivate and manage your energy — I invite students to visualize storing their energy in their lower dantien — the area below the belly button that represents a reservoir of vital energy or qi. You are responsible for tending to this energy through mindful choices about how you eat, think, act, and about who you invite into your world. You can restore and replenish depleted energy through proper nourishment, mindful movement, and protective boundaries that protect you from difficult interactions.

Have you noticed how certain encounters leave you exhausted or even dizzy? Perhaps it's that friend who perpetually dwells in drama, the relative whose subtle judgments diminish your spirit, or even those crowded social gatherings that somehow leave you feeling strangely disconnected and off-center. These are not mere coincidences; they are clear evidence of your energetic sensitivity.

Your personal energy field (some refer to it as your aura) functions as a sophisticated antenna, constantly receiving and processing the invisible currents that surround us. These energetic imprints come from everywhere — the chronic complainer, the tense atmosphere of a crowded room, or even the residual heaviness in physical spaces where conflict has occurred. While some individuals seem naturally shielded from these influences, many of us — particularly women — possess a heightened sensitivity that makes us more receptive to others' energetic states, both nurturing and depleting. This sensitivity calls for intentional protection of our energetic boundaries — a skill every Empress must master.

I recall a friendship that illustrates this principle perfectly. This woman presented herself as kind and supportive, yet could transform in an instant, directing unexpected hostility toward others. In her company, my body would constantly signal me with muscles tension and headaches, physical signals of energetic intrusion. Though I wanted to challenge her negativity, I recognized the overwhelming energy at play and chose to protect myself rather than engage.

During this time, I was deepening my studies in energy work and intuitive development, exploring the complexities of the human auric field. As a Reiki practitioner working with others' energy systems to identify and address imbalances, I came to understand an essential truth: we must first master the art of energetic self-care, clearing accumulated energetic residue that naturally adheres during interactions.

Your body speaks a sophisticated language of energy. Often, you absorb others' emotional states without conscious awareness until physical symptoms manifest — unexplained fatigue, sudden mood shifts, or a vague sense of discomfort. When you're attuned to your own energetic state, you might perceive these subtle imbalances sooner, sensing when something feels off. Developing protective practices allows us to remain compassionate without absorbing the emotional weight of others' experiences.

In my own journey with energy sensitivity, I discovered the transformative power of energetic visualization — creating a protective shield when engaging with individuals I recognized as energetic vampires (often called this for their unconscious ability to drain vitality from those around them). This practice is simple yet remarkably effective: you visualize a luminous bubble or white light surrounding your entire being, containing your energy while preventing unwanted external influences from penetrating.

I put this technique to the test with the friend I mentioned earlier. When I began practicing this visualization before our interactions, the results were immediate. Our conversations gradually shortened and, eventually, the dynamic of the friendship shifted. While we remained cordial, the intensity of her energetic pull diminished significantly. The relationship naturally found more balance, one where I no longer felt depleted after our encounters. Rather than experiencing this change as a loss, I felt a profound sense of relief and reclaimed energy.

As energetically sensitive beings, we can absorb the emotional states of anyone within our environment, especially those closest to us. I've experienced this countless times when my husband enters a room and I suddenly find myself mirroring his frustration without explanation. Only later, when he mentions challenges at work or a difficult interaction does the realization dawn: "Ah, I was absorbing his energy as my own."

This sensitivity, however, doesn't mean we must constantly maintain energetic barriers against everyone we encounter. Discernment is key. You can selectively employ protective practices when you notice your energy change in specific environments or around particular individuals. This is when you might invoke your protective visualization, enabling you to remain present while maintaining your energetic sovereignty. This practice, which I call **Empress Protection**, represents the delicate art of maintaining your energetic boundaries while remaining open to genuine connection. It embodies discernment rather than disconnection. An Empress recognizes that sensitivity is not a vulnerability to overcome but a gift to develop and protect.

Energetic Sovereignty: Your Divine Right

Energetic sovereignty is the divine right of every Empress to govern her own energetic domain. You rule your kingdom with authority and grace, and you have the absolute right to determine what energies may enter your field and what must remain outside your borders. True sovereignty means recognizing that you alone hold the scepter of your energetic realm. No one — regardless of their relationship to you, their needs, or their demands — has the right to deplete your vital energy. Maintaining your energetic sovereignty isn't selfish, it's spiritual leadership.

Women are often naturally more energetically sensitive than men, a gift that can become a burden without proper understanding. Our nervous systems are designed to attune to others — and has long served us in caring for children and nurturing relationships. Additionally, many women have been socialized to be emotional caretakers, absorbing others' pain and trying to fix what's broken around them. While this compassion is beautiful, without sovereignty, it becomes a pathway to depletion rather than healing.

In our Empress years, this pattern becomes even more costly. We may find ourselves caring for aging parents while supporting adult children, leaving little energy for our own dreams and desires. Yet this is precisely when we need our energy most—to pursue new passions, share our wisdom, and create the legacy we want to leave.

For many women, life becomes a constant cycle of giving until empty, then struggling to refill from an already depleted well. Without energetic sovereignty, you may find yourself constantly exhausted despite adequate sleep, unable to distinguish between your emotions and others', saying yes when every fiber of your being wants to say no, feeling responsible for managing everyone else's emotional state, and losing touch with your own desires and intuitive guidance.

When you claim your energetic sovereignty, several powerful transformations occur:

- You become the conscious gatekeeper of your energy, rather than an unconscious absorber of whatever surrounds you.

- You develop discernment about which connections nourish you and which diminish your light.

- You honor your sensitivity as a gift of perception rather than treating it as a vulnerability to overcome.

- You recognize energy exchanges in all interactions and consciously choose which to engage in.

- You stop apologizing for protecting what is rightfully yours.

The Empress who has claimed her energetic sovereignty walks differently in the world. She engages with genuine compassion while maintaining her center. She offers her presence as a gift, not as an obligation. She understands that maintaining her energetic field isn't just self-care; it's the foundation of her ability to serve her highest purpose and contribute her unique wisdom.

Empress Protection Practices

RECOGNIZING WHEN PROTECTION IS NEEDED

Developing awareness of your energetic well-being provides crucial guidance for when protection is needed. To maintain the energetic balance of an Empress, tune into when these occur:

- Sudden mood shifts after being around certain people
- Unexplained fatigue or anxiety
- Unexplained physical symptoms like headaches or tension
- Persistent people-pleasing at your own expense
- Difficulty sleeping despite feeling exhausted
- Feeling overwhelmed by crowds or noise

When you notice these signs, you're not being "too sensitive." This is your inner wisdom speaking. Your auric field is asking you for attention. Remember, an Empress honors these messages rather than dismissing them.

THE EMPRESS'S SHIELD

Close your eyes and take three deep breaths. Visualize yourself surrounded by a luminous protective bubble of golden light. Make this technique part of your regular routine — before leaving your home or attending events where the energy might be intense. Through this practice, you are consciously using your intention to protect your auric field. This isn't just visualization; it's creating an energetic boundary that honors both yourself and others.

CRYSTAL ALLIES

Keep protective stones close by — in your pocket, worn as jewelry, or placed in your sacred space. You can select any crystal that you feel called to work with, trusting your intuition to guide you to what you need. These aren't mere decorations; they're part of your energetic crown jewels.

Protective crystals include:

Black tourmaline: serves as your guardian against negative energies

Amethyst: offers spiritual protection and enhances intuition

Hematite: grounds your energy and creates a protective shield

Obsidian: absorbs negative energy and provides deep protection

Labradorite: protects your aura and enhances psychic abilities

Garnet: provides grounding protection and boosts confidence

Tiger's eye: offers protection while maintaining mental clarity

Cleansing crystals include:

Selenite: (named after moon goddess Selene) bathes your aura in purifying light

Clear quartz: amplifies positive energy and clears negativity

Smoky quartz: transmutes negative energy into positive

Fluorite: clears mental fog and negative thought patterns

Citrine: cleanses negative energy and attracts abundance

Aquamarine: promotes emotional clarity and peaceful energy

Rose quartz: heals emotional wounds and promotes self-love

An Empress values her right to say no when necessary. You don't need to attend every gathering, solve every problem, or be available to everyone. Setting boundaries isn't selfish; it's necessary for maintaining the energy you need to serve your highest purpose.

YOUR ROYAL INVITATION

Now that you understand the principles of energetic sovereignty, here are a few more practices that you can choose from to integrate into your daily realm:

DAILY REGAL RITUALS:

- Begin each morning with 5-10 minutes of mindful breathing to center yourself.
- Clear your space daily with selenite, sage, or simply by opening windows and setting intention.
- Take regular nature baths — even 10 minutes outdoors daily helps Mother Earth restore you.
- Practice qigong, dancing, or gentle movement to keep your energy flowing throughout your body.
- End each day by consciously releasing others' energies through intention or visualization.

ENERGY MAINTENANCE PRACTICES:

- Stay hydrated with intention; sip water throughout the day, perhaps infused with revitalizing herbs or fruits.
- Create an energy inventory at day's end, noting which interactions filled your cup and which depleted it.
- Limit exposure to draining activities (excessive news consumption, dramatic people, social media).
- Schedule at least fifteen minutes of sacred solitude daily; mark it in your calendar as a non-negotiable appointment with yourself.

WHEN FEELING OVERWHELMED (GROUNDING PRACTICES):

- Place your bare feet on the earth for 5-10 minutes daily.
- Visualize roots extending from your feet deep into the earth's core.
- End showers with thirty seconds of cool water while visualizing negative energy washing away.
- Hold a hematite or smoky quartz crystal while setting intention for stability.

SACRED SPACE & DIGITAL PROTECTION:

- Use sea salt in the corners of your throne room to absorb negative energy.
- Place crystals strategically throughout your sacred space to amplify protection.
- Set time boundaries for social media and news consumption.
- Create a thirty-minute buffer between screen time and sleep.
- Practice a ten-second centering breath before checking messages or emails.

Remember, dear Empress, establishing energetic boundaries isn't about disconnection; it's about conscious discernment that allows your wisdom to flourish. When you protect your energy field with intention and care, you preserve the vital force needed to share your unique gifts with the world.

Your energy is your kingdom. Rule it wisely.

CORONATION

Dear Empress,

As we reach the final pages of this journey together, know this: this is not an ending — it's your coronation.

You have traveled through these chapters not as a passive reader, but as an active participant in your own transformation. You have walked a sacred path, awakened your divine power, reclaimed your sovereignty, and learned to protect the sacred energy that is uniquely yours. You've faced the outdated narratives, dismantled limiting beliefs, and chosen — again and again — to rise.

The path from crone to crown isn't just about changing a label — it's about fundamentally shifting how you see yourself and how you move through the world. You are not invisible. You are not diminishing. You are not meant to fade into the background of your own life. You are an Empress, radiant with the accumulated wisdom of your journey, powerful in ways that only come from having lived, loved, struggled, and emerged stronger.

Perhaps you picked up this book because something inside you resonated with the title. Maybe you felt overlooked or dismissed one too many times. Maybe you looked in the mirror and didn't recognize the woman staring back at you. Or perhaps you simply sensed there was more to this chapter of life than what our culture has led us to believe.

Whatever brought you here, I want you to know something important: That feeling you have — that quiet voice whispering that you deserve more? That's not wishful thinking — that's your Empress energy calling you home to your throne.

For too long, we've been told stories about aging that simply don't serve us. We've been shown images of women fading into the background, becoming less visible, less powerful, less everything. And I'm here to tell you that's complete nonsense.

The Eight Pillars of Empress Energy we explored together — sovereignty, transformation, self-care, intuitive wisdom, energy protection, abundance, forgiveness, and community — aren't just beautiful concepts to contemplate. They're practical pathways to living as the Empress you truly are. When you step into your sovereignty, protect your energy, honor your intuition, and gather with other Empresses, you create ripples that extend far beyond yourself.

I'm not saying it's always easy. Some days the old stories creep back in. Some days the mirror seems unkind. Some days the world tries to make you feel invisible. I get it — I've been there too. But here's what I know for sure: Once you've glimpsed your Empress nature, once you've felt what it's like to sit on your throne, there's no going back to the old narratives.

You might be wondering, what now? Now, dear Empress, you practice. You return to the Royal Invitations that stirred something in your soul — those sacred practices that will become the foundation of your daily reign. Create and protect your sacred space. Speak your truth, even if your voice quivers. Practice those morning declarations that remind you of your worth. Build your circle of radiant women who rise with you. These aren't just exercises — they're your royal tools, designed to keep you anchored in your Empress energy even when the world tries to pull you back into old patterns.

As you close this book and step fully into your Empress energy, remember that your throne awaits — not as a destination, but as a way of being. Your sovereignty isn't something you achieve; it's something you claim, moment by moment, choice by choice.

The world needs what you have to offer. It needs your wisdom that can only come from having walked your unique path. It needs your voice that carries the authority of lived experience. It needs your light that has learned to shine even in the darkness.

You are not too old to begin again. You are not too late to the party. You are right on time — perfectly, divinely, magnificently on time.

Remember, when you stand in your Empress energy, you're not just changing your own story — you're creating a new vision of what's possible for women everywhere. When a younger woman sees you owning your power, speaking your truth, and shining brightly without apology, she sees someone who is truly sovereign — a woman who inspires her to believe in her own sacred worth. She begins to look forward to her own Empress years rather than dreading the passage of time.

So go ahead — claim your throne. Treat yourself like royalty. Straighten your crown. And whenever you need a reminder of your magnificence, return to these pages. I'll be here, Empress to Empress, reminding you of who you truly are.

You are now part of a growing sisterhood of Empresses around the world — women who refuse to be invisible, who claim their worth, and who understand that their wisdom years are their most powerful years. When you see another woman struggling to find her voice, offer her encouragement. When you encounter a sister whose crown sits askew, gently help her straighten it. This is how we rise together.

Together, we are not just changing the story. We are rewriting the script for generations of women to come.

The Empress Declaration

Place your hand over your heart, take a deep breath, and speak these truths out loud:

I am an Empress Rising. I honor the path I have walked, the wisdom I carry, and the power I embody.

I release all narratives that diminish me and embrace the truth of who I am.

My voice matters, my energy is sacred, and my presence is a gift to this world.

I sit upon the throne of my life — sovereign, radiant, and unapologetically myself.

I am not done blooming. I am not done creating. I am not done becoming. I am just beginning.

I rise not alone, but with other Empresses — and together, we rewrite the story for every woman who follows.

I AM AN EMPRESS. AND I RISE.

Take a moment to thank your past self for every choice that brought you to this moment of awakening. Thank your present self for having the courage to claim your power. Thank your future self for all she is about to become.

This ceremony marks not an end, but a beginning. Your Empress energy will continue to evolve and deepen with each day you choose to honor it. Some days you'll feel your crown slipping, and that's okay. Simply straighten it and carry on. Some days you'll forget your power, and that's human. Simply remember and reclaim it.

Your Empress journey continues.

Before you close this book, look around your life — your kingdom. Feel the quiet strength of a woman who knows who she is. This is the beginning of your reign. Straighten your crown. Take your throne. Let every step you take from here be rooted in the truth of your worth.

You are an Empress — wise, radiant, and ready for all that is still to come.

With sovereignty and grace,

Rose

ABOUT THE AUTHOR

Rose Wippich is an energy alchemist, Reiki Master Teacher, mentor, qigong, and yoga instructor who guides women to reclaim their sovereignty in what she calls their "Empress years." After navigating many of life's profound challenges, including breast cancer at 49, Rose underwent a spiritual awakening that transformed her approach to aging, healing, and personal empowerment.

Rose's revolutionary philosophy reframes aging as expansion rather than diminishment, calling women to abandon society's limiting narratives and step into their "Empress years" with confidence, grace, and unapologetic power. Her teaching combines fierce compassion with practical tools, helping women establish energetic boundaries, practice forgiveness as liberation, and discover the radiant authority that emerges when they stop shrinking and start shining.

Having alchemized her own life experiences into wisdom, Rose now guides other women through the sacred art of transformation. She helps them cut energetic cords that no longer serve, claim their sovereign space, and embrace their role as wisdom-keepers and leaders. Rose embodies the very Empress energy she teaches—deeply grounded in practical wisdom while connected to higher guidance, radiating the authentic power that comes from a life fully lived and consciously transformed.

When she's not teaching, writing, or podcasting, Rose can be found practicing qigong, pulling oracle cards, spending time with her husband and twin boys, or mentoring other women on their spiritual journeys. She believes that when one woman rises into her power, she creates ripples that help lift all women.

Empress Rising is her first book, born from her deep desire to help women rewrite the narrative around aging and step boldly into their most magnificent years.

To discover more about Rose Wippich, visit www.rosewippich.com or scan the QR Code below.

www.ingramcontent.com/pod-product-compliance
Lightning Source LLC
Chambersburg PA
CBHW021635120626
46545CB00002B/551